IMAGES
of America

AROUND EBARB AND
THE TOLEDO BEND

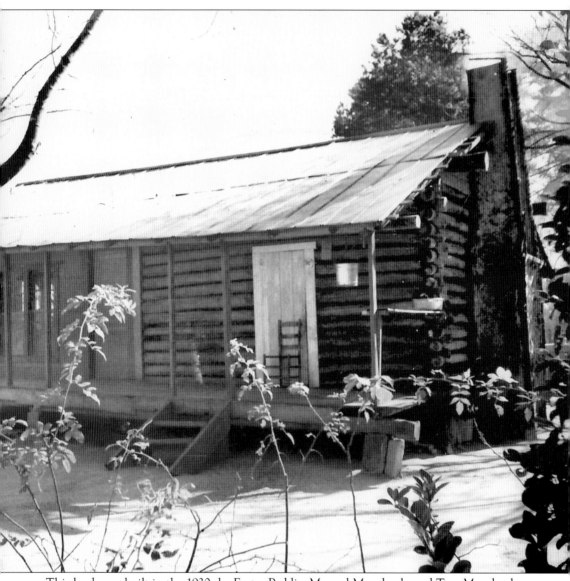

This log house built in the 1930s by Foster Paddie, Manuel Manshack, and Tom Manshack was the first home of Manuel and Maybell Manshack. Two of their children, Sam Harvey and Patricia Ann, were born in this house. Later Tom Manshack, brother of Manuel, moved into this house and raised his family in this log cabin. This picture was taken in December 1968. (Courtesy of Lois Manshack.)

ON THE COVER: When the Toledo Bend Reservoir was created for the purpose of a water supply, hydroelectric power generation, and recreation in the 1960s, it covered some rural roads used by local people to get to church—St. Ann's in Ebarb. Fr. William J. Pearce, pastor of St. Ann's, helped parishioners get to church activities. He is seen in the photograph ferrying children to religion classes. Pictured are, from front to back, (first row) Herman Procell, Johnny Manshack, and James Olin Manshack; (second row) Jimmy Lee Manshack, Marilyn Procell, and Fr. William J. Pierce; (third row) James Procell, Kathleen Procell, Billy Wayne Procell, and Thomas Ray Procell. (Courtesy of Joe [Dee] Procell.)

IMAGES
of America

AROUND EBARB AND THE TOLEDO BEND

Mary Lucille Rivers
and Travis Ebarb Jr.

ARCADIA
PUBLISHING

Published by Arcadia Publishing
Charleston SC, Chicago IL, Portsmouth NH, San Francisco CA

Printed in the United States of America

Library of Congress Catalog Card Number: 2006935809

For all general information contact Arcadia Publishing at:
Telephone 843-853-2070
Fax 843-853-0044
E-mail sales@arcadiapublishing.com
For customer service and orders:
Toll-Free 1-888-313-2665

Visit us on the Internet at www.arcadiapublishing.com

*This book is dedicated to Richard Travis Ebarb Sr. and
Patricia Ann (Manshack) Ebarb for the love and devotion
that they have shown each other and their family throughout the years.*

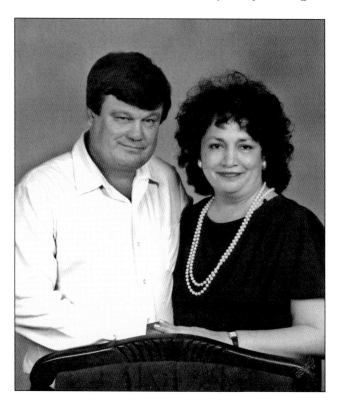

CONTENTS

ACKNOWLEDGMENTS

Many sources were utilized during the collection and assembly of this pictorial history book. When available, we obtained and made use of as many primary sources of information as possible. In the event that a primary source could not be obtained, secondary sources of information were utilized.

Oral tradition is yet another valuable source of historical information. Interestingly enough, every photograph had a story to be told by its present owner. Quite often, fact and fiction were so interwoven it was difficult to discern what was true and what wasn't. Important information, which greatly helped in this clarification process, was gathered from 150 unpublished interviews of tribal elders, conducted from 1982 to 1984 by Mary Van Rheenan and Janet Shoemaker. We are indebted to Mary Linn Wernet at the Cammie G. Henry Research Center for allowing us use of these records.

Other sources of information were Old Spanish Censuses from 1795 to 1835; Louisiana and Texas censuses; U.S. censuses; court records, property records, wills, and marriage and death records; Carl Dilbeck's *Sabine Parish Cemeteries*; records from St. Joseph's Catholic Church in Zwolle, Louisiana, St. Ann's Catholic Church in Ebarb, Louisiana, St. John's Catholic Church in Many, Louisiana, Sacred Heart Catholic Church in Nacogdoches, Texas, and Immaculate Conception Church in Natchitoches, Louisiana; *History of St. Joseph's Catholic Church* by Elvera Procell and Phyllis Murdock and its revised edition by Martha Foshee; *Sabine Index*; *Shreveport Times*; and *Daily Sentinel*.

To the following, who have conducted many years of research, we thank you: late Alene Wright, Cody Bruce, Martha Foshee, Bill Bowien, Michael LeRoy, Virginia Malmay, Pati and Doug Laroux, Paul Ferguson, Bob and Wilma Valentine, Penny and Jerry Rivers, Mary Martinez, Tommy Bolton, Donald Lester Sepulvado, Dr. Hiram F. Gregory, Ernest Rodriguez, Theresa Rivers, Ione Durr, late Elvera Procell, and Carl Dilbeck.

We would also like to thank Michael LeRoy for scanning and rescanning the pictures, Marie Polk, Kathryn Boudreaux, Karen Montgomery, James Pratt, Dr. F. E. Abernethy, Rebecca Morris at Sabine Parish Library, Dollie Knippers at Sabine Parish Courthouse, Tommy Bolton and Virginia Malmay for checking articles for historical accuracy, Corneal Cox, Doug Ireland, Frank Dutton, and Martin Crooks.

INTRODUCTION

The Ebarb–Zwolle–Toledo Bend area of Louisiana has a colorful and exciting past but has been largely ignored by historians of Anglo-American traditions. For centuries, this region was home to the French, Spanish, and many tribes of Native Americans. Their unique contribution to culture, agriculture, businesses, churches, schools, medicines, and entertainment has been undocumented and unrecognized.

This area of land between Natchitoches, Louisiana, and Nacogdoches, Texas, (called "the Neutral Zone," "No Man's Land," or "Sabine Free State") was also home to various groups of outlaws from surrounding areas. The Spanish and French squabbled for years over the ownership of these lands. The federal government entered into this dispute. In 1819, the Adams-Onis Treaty established a permanent border between the United States and Spanish territories and effectively opened the area to settlement by Anglo-Americans.

The history of this area presently known for its Tamale Fiesta and Forestry Festival can be traced back to the Mound Indians. Remnants of the mounds used as burial grounds or other religious ceremonies as well as protection from storms can still be found along Bayou Scie and Bayou San Miguel. Many centuries later, the Caddo Federation of Indians occupied this area of north central Louisiana along the Sabine and Red Rivers. Twenty-five different tribes made up this confederation. They consisted of three different groups: the Hasinai confederation of the Tejas, who were very friendly; the Kadohadacho proper; and the confederacy of the Wichita, known primarily as the Ouachitas. Those living in Sabine Parish were later called Adai.

The Caddo were not fierce and warlike when compared to some other Native American groups but usually were satisfied with hunting and various ceremonies. The women's job consisted of raising corn, pumpkins, gourds, watermelons, squash, and tobacco. The Caddo were skilled in hunting with the bow and arrow. They also excelled in basketry and pottery making. Their arrows, spears, and tomahawks can still be found in fields and hillsides across Sabine Parish.

When the Spanish fort, Los Adaes, was abruptly closed in 1773, the soldiers and their families were forced to hurriedly leave and make the long, arduous trip to San Antonio, Texas. Don Antonio Gil Y'barbo assumed a leadership role, trying to overcome exposure, famine, and fatigue. Many of the weak, the elderly, the sick, and the very young died and were buried along the way. Approximately 167 people eventually arrived in San Antonio, Texas.

Rather than abandon their homes, many of these people (some who had been born at Los Adaes) fled into the forests or to nearby Native American friends. Some of these people, particularly the Y'barbos, came to the Ebarb area. They settled there and their descendants remain there today. The Ebarb School (one of the only Native American schools in the state of Louisiana) and the St. Ann's Catholic Church of Ebarb attest to the strong work and religious ethnic. Nearly 100 Ebarb families were listed in the Zwolle-Ebarb telephone directory in 2006.

These people, who settled at Ebarb, rightly so had a distrust of the government and many did not appear in the early 1840 census. These early records (some in Spanish) were taken to San Antonio and Mexico City. Some were lost, not properly recorded, or disappeared over time.

The descendants of these early Spanish, French, and Native American people still live in the Zwolle-Ebarb area today. Their vast numbers extend to probably all of the 50 states. The Choctaw-Apache community of Ebarb, one of the largest American Indian tribes in the state, was incorporated in 1977, is recognized by the State of Louisiana, and is actively pursuing federal recognition.

Early family names, some Americanized, remain listed in the telephone directory in 2006: Ebarb (Y'barbo), Rivers (Del Rio), Sepulvado (Sepulvada), Leone (Samuel dit Lyon), Manshack (Manchaca), Martinez, Parrie (Parrillo), Bebee (Brevel), Ezernack (Sarnac), Meshell (Micheli), Paddie (Padilla), Procell (Procella), Cordova, Remedies (Ramirez), Bison (Beson), Garcie (Garcia), Laroux (Rond), Malmay (Bermea), Mora, and Castie (Castillo).

Their descendants include many professionals: doctors, nurses, attorneys, teachers, and accountants. Today many of the local names can be traced back to Spanish, French, Indian, or English ancestry. Most of the Spanish influence in Sabine Parish was brought in via the El Camino Real, the "King's Highway." This diverse community is a hodgepodge, a mixture of these people and their culture.

Another group of Native Americans connected to this area of Louisiana are the Lipan Apaches. They were skilled at warfare and talented with horses. The Spanish tried to convert them to Christianity but had little success. The Lipans would raid the Spanish settlements. As a result, campaigns against the Lipans lasted well into the 19th century. The Wichita, Pawnee, and Caddo all participated in selling Apache captives. Eventually these Apache slaves found themselves in both the Spanish and French settlements around this area of Northwest Louisiana, especially in Natchitoches. Natchitoches was the main place of trade for Native American slavery. These slaves were used for laborers, interpreters, guides, and household workers. Many of the women became wives of both the French and Spanish. Their children were known as "Metis" by the French and "Mestizo" by the Spanish. Many of the present-day occupants of Sabine Parish are descendants, "Mestizos."

Around the time that Nacogdoches was settled, the Spanish government decided to entice several tribes away from the English influences east of the Mississippi River. The Spanish government invited the Choctaw and other eastern tribes to cross the Mississippi River and settle in Louisiana.

The Choctaw were not welcome in many places because they would raid, hunt, and attack other groups already living here. One group of Choctaw settled the Sabine River area. After the federal government acquired the Louisiana territory in 1803, tension arose between Spain and the United States. Consequently, a "Neutral Strip" was established between Rio Hondo near Los Adaes and the Sabine River. This area became a haven for outlaws, runaway slaves, honest farmers, and various groups of Native Americans. Many bands of Choctaw came into the area around this time. Some Choctaws formed communities in the Sabine area, became permanent settlers, and later mixed with the local population. Today in Sabine Parish, a large group of people are descendants of the Caddo, Apache, and Choctaw. Throughout the 1800s, the Choctaws in Oklahoma encouraged the Louisiana and Mississippi Choctaws to join them.

In 1838, many of the Spanish–Native American groups in the Nacogdoches area rebelled against the Anglos who were taking their lands. Some of the local people joined a Mestizo, Vincente Cordova, to rebel against the English. When what was known as the "Cordovan Rebellion" ended, those who had participated in it had to leave or be prosecuted for treason. Thus, we see many leaving for Mexico or joining their relatives east of the Sabine River. Brothers Juan, Jose, and Cayetano Martinez left and settled in Sabine Parish. Manuel Ybarbo and his children also chose to leave. The Garcia family, along with Jose Antonio Sepulvada and his wife, Guadalupe Chavana, came to Sabine Parish.

One

St. Joseph's
Catholic Church

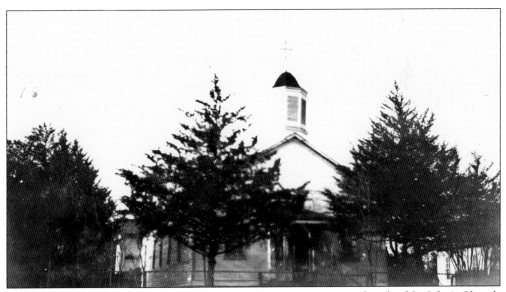

This church at St. Joseph's in Zwolle, Louisiana, began as a mission church of St. John's Church in Many, Louisiana. It became an independent establishment in 1881. Rev. J. M. Ledreux became its resident pastor (1881–1884) followed by Fr. J. A. Aubree (1884–1897). The church remained in service until it was replaced by a modern structure built by Msgr. Robert C. Friend in 1957. (Courtesy of the Roy Procell collection.)

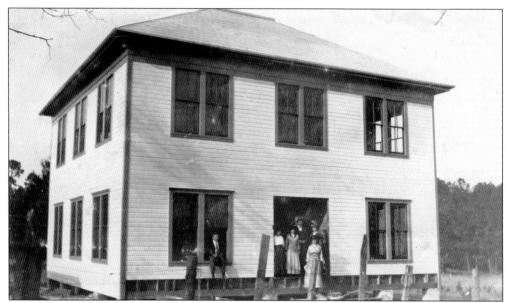

St. Joseph Catholic School was built during the administration of Fr. John Van Bokhoven in 1915. The convent was a two-story frame building that served as the sisters' home and the school. One large classroom, three bedrooms, and a study were on the second floor. One large classroom, a parlor that served as a music room, a kitchen, and a dining room were on the first floor. (Courtesy of the Roy Procell collection.)

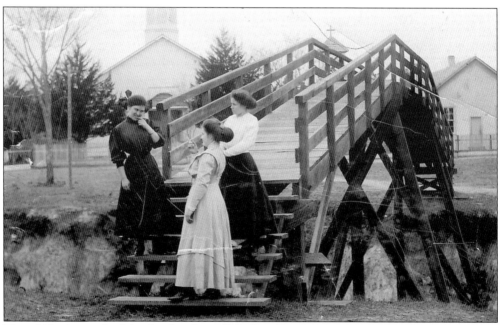

This old bridge was built by the church to allow churchgoers access to St. Joseph's Church. Local parishioners enjoy a Sunday afternoon in front of the church and the Church Hall. In the early days, families would travel by wagon and camp out at the foot of the bridge. (Courtesy of the Roy Procell collection.)

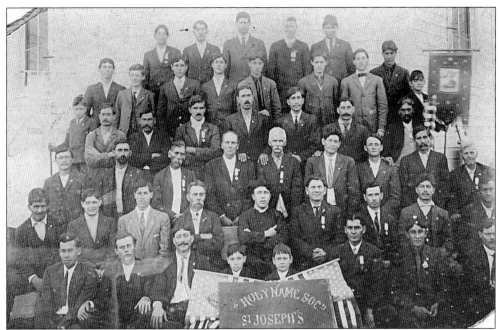

The Holy Name Society at St. Joseph's is pictured in 1912. From left to right are (first row) Jeff Castillo, George Wethey, Phillip Ebarb, Patrick Ebarb, Sam Cartinez, Joseph Ezernack, Steve Procell, and Henry Pipps; (second row) Joseph Ebarb, John Ezernack, William Ebarb, W. M. Ebarb, Fr. Francis Van Haver, John Ferguson, Joseph Ezernack, Benjamin Knight, and Hosea Procell; (third row) Joe Pipps, Simon Malmay, Manuel Cartinez, Lou Leone, Sam Ezernack, Sevedo Ebarb, Wesley Ebarb, Con Procell, and John Ezernack; (fourth row) Johnny Malmay, Tom Meshell, Frank Ebarb, Dee Malmay, Tom Malmay, Dash Procell, Jessie Ebarb, and Horace Paddie; (fifth row) Richard Laroux, Anthony Kezerle, John Paddie, Joseph Ebarb, Prude Remedies, Willie Ezernack, Paul Ebarb, Henry Ebarb, and Sam Malmay; (sixth row) Jim Ezernack, John Nigreville, Abraham Ebarb, Martin Ebarb, and Phillip Procell. (Courtesy of Marie Polk.)

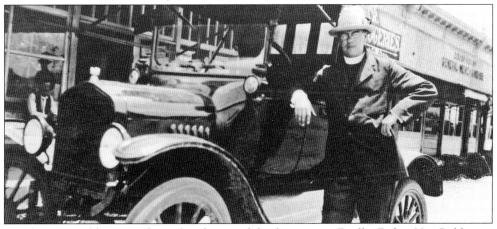

Fr. John Van Bokhoven is shown beside one of the first cars in Zwolle. Father Van Bokhoven was born in Holland in 1885. He built the first Catholic school, which opened in 1915 staffed by four Sisters of Divine Providence. Unfortunately, Zwolle was the father's only pastorate as he died of a ruptured appendix in 1932. He is buried in St. Joseph Cemetery. (Courtesy of the Roy Procell collection.)

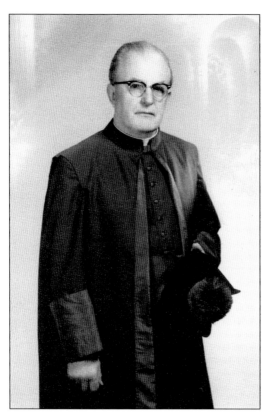

Bishop Charles P. Greco appointed Msgr. Robert C. Friend pastor of St. Joseph's in March 1944. His pastorship included three missions: St. Ann's in Ebarb, St. Catherine's near Sulphur Springs, and a church at Round Lake. During his 31-year tenure at St. Joseph's, Father Friend redid the entire church complex, including the rectory, a new church, school, and administration building–convent. He also added to the cemetery. (Courtesy of Kathryn Boudreaux.)

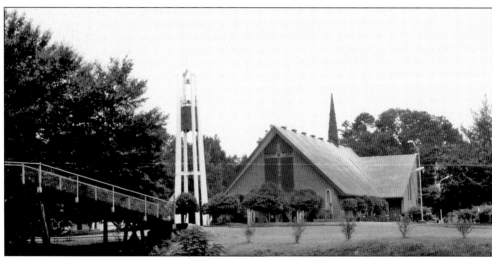

This present St. Joseph Catholic Church, designed by Msgr. Robert C. Friend, was built to replace the old one built in 1881. Estimated at the time to be worth $200,000, it was dedicated on April 28, 1957, by Bishop Charles Greco. A solemn mass followed with Father Friend as celebrant and Fr. George Martinez of Monroe, a native of Zwolle, as sub-deacon. (Courtesy of Martin Crooks.)

Two

EBARB COMMUNITY CHURCHES

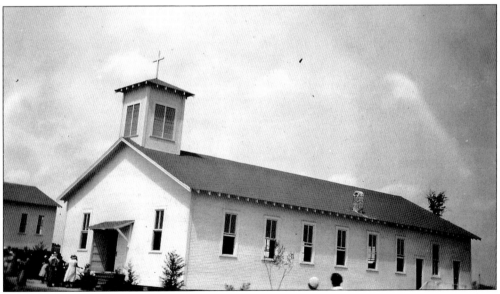

This church at St. Ann's was built on land donated by Mary (Sepulvado) Ebarb. It was built in 1935 and became a mission of St. Joseph's Church in Zwolle. In 1953, Msgr. Robert C. Friend, pastor of St. Joseph's, added a rectory to the north end of the church, and in 1955, St. Ann's became an independent church. (Courtesy of John C. and Carla Ebarb.)

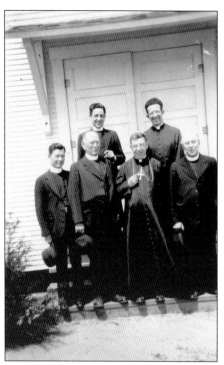

On April 1, 1935, these prelates met to dedicate the new St. Ann's Church in Ebarb. From left to right are (first row) Fr. Joseph Fortin, Father Green, Bishop Daniel F. Desmond, and Fr. Francis Van Haver; (second row) Father Cassidy and Fr. James Howard. The church was built on land donated by Mary (Sepulvado) Ebarb. The church was a 40-by-80-foot building with a seating capacity of 500. (Courtesy of the Roy Procell collection.)

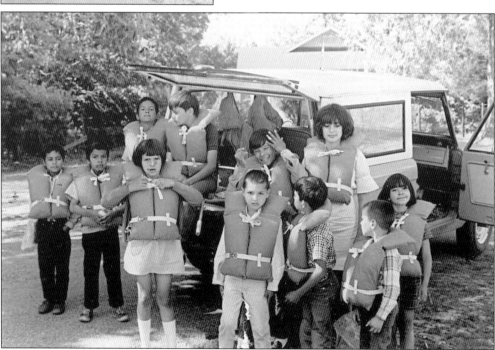

Waiting on Father Pierce and getting ready to "cross the creek" to go back home after Catechism were these patient children. From left to right are (first row) Billy Wayne Procell, Gilbert Procell, Debra Lopez, James Manshack Jr., Herman Procell, Johnny Ray Manshack, and Hilda Procell; (second row) James Procell, Terry Joe Lopez, Thomas Ray Procell, and Marilyn Procell. (Courtesy of Joe [Dee] Procell.)

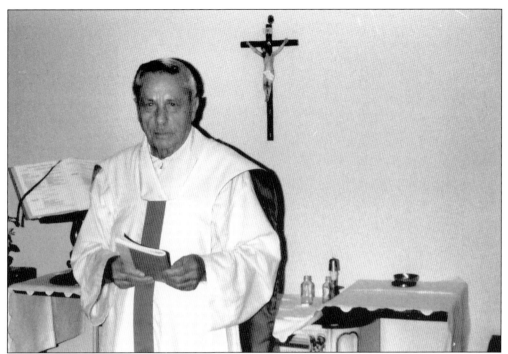

Fr. Luis Antiltz was born on March 10, 1901, in Watertown, South Dakota. He was an orphan at an early age when both parents died of tuberculosis. After his orphanage years, he entered the seminary in 1924 and was ordained on June 14, 1930. He served eight years at St. Ann's Catholic Church in Ebarb. He is buried under the cross in St. Ann's Catholic Cemetery. He is the only priest buried in this cemetery. (Courtesy of Raymond L. and Joan Ebarb.)

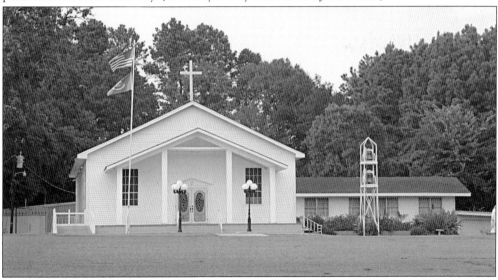

St. Ann's Church in Ebarb is a modern, air-conditioned, renovated church. In the summer of 2005, it was made into a quasi-parish when Fr. Kenneth Williams retired. The priests, Fr. Tim Hurd and Fr. Mark Franklin, assist in providing services for the congregation. The church and school have been the focal point of activities for the community for many years. (Courtesy of Martin Crooks.)

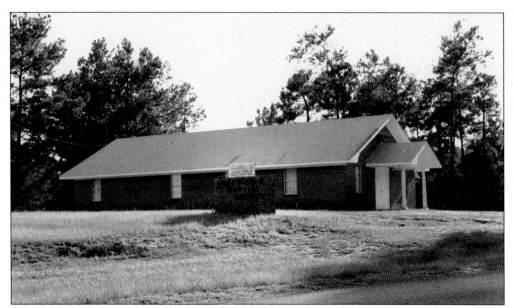

The Lakeview Baptist Church was built in 1967. It is located near the John Brown Curve, which has been the scene of many bad wrecks and is the source of local legends. The Forest View Church building was moved from the present-day Bill Ebarb Road to its current location. Frank Chance was pastor before Paul Ferrant. (Courtesy of Martin Crooks.)

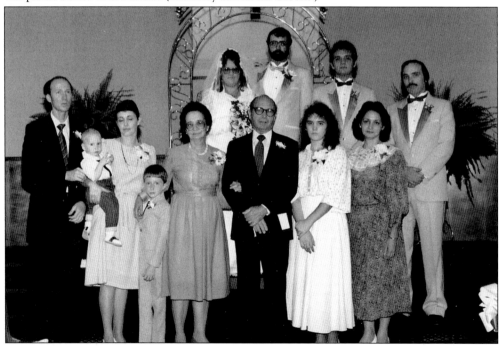

The Paul and Joy Ferrant family came to the Ebarb community in 1959. Rev. Paul Ferrant served as a minister of the Baptist church, and Joy taught at Ebarb High School for 23 years. The Ferrant family from left to right is (first row) Jack Harp, Bradley Harp, Verena Harp, Wesley Harp, Joy Ferrant, Paul Ferrant, Angelia Ferrant, and Merle Ferrant; (second row) Ann Ferrant, Dale Ferrant, Mark Ferrant, and Wayne Ferrant. (Courtesy of Paul and Joy Ferrant.)

Three

ZWOLLE AND NOBLE SCHOOLS

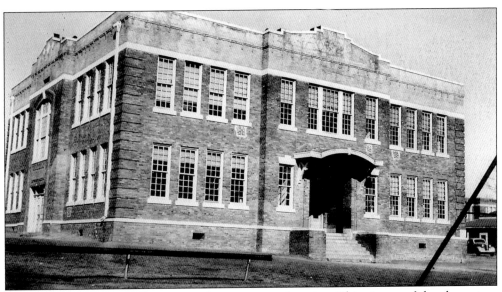

In 1913, the Zwolle School was moved to its present location. This picture of the elementary school was taken in 1947. After World War II, Woodrow Salter served as principal from 1947 to 1970. Under Salter's leadership, the present auditorium and gymnasium were built. (Courtesy of Travis Ebarb Jr.)

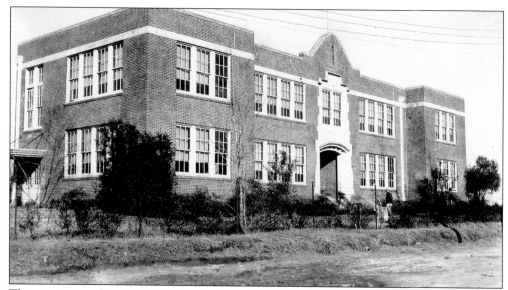

This is a picture of Zwolle High School taken in 1947. It was built in 1930 because the student body had outgrown its buildings. It was a two-story brick building with many windows for ventilation. Several generations of Zwolle students attended this school. In 1950, the 12th grade was added. (Courtesy of Travis Ebarb Jr.)

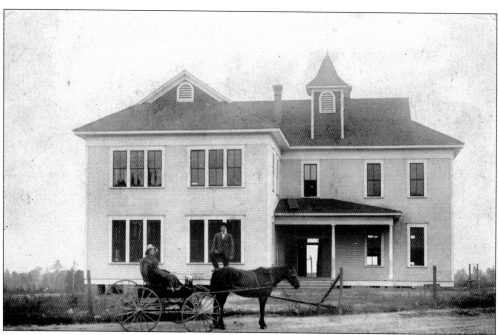

Noble, Louisiana, was originally located on the Kansas City Southern Railroad between Bayou San Patricio and Bayou San Miguel. The settlement of this section of Sabine Parish dates back to the 1830s. This early school was located at Hicks' Camp. Its first teachers were B. Godfrey and A. Hubler. The Mustangs were Noble's mascot. (Courtesy of Marie Polk.)

Four

EBARB HIGH SCHOOL

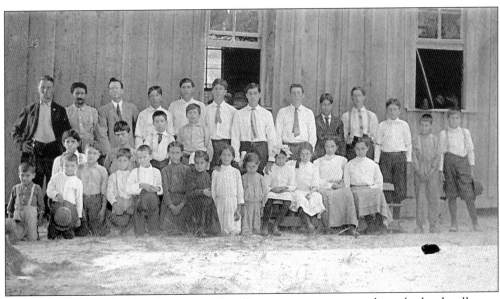

This picture is Ebarb School's second schoolhouse, a one-room standing-plank schoolhouse. Students pictured from left to right are (first row) Billy Ebarb, Clarence Ebarb, three unidentified, Blanche Ebarb (in a black dress), Edna Ebarb (in a black dress), three unidentified, Maggie Ebarb, Lucy Ebarb, and Fannie Ebarb; (second row) two unidentified, Pat Ebarb, and unidentified; (third row) William Ebarb, unidentified, ? Pilcher (the teacher), Walter Ebarb, Bill Ebarb Jr., Cary Ebarb, Paul Ebarb, Martin Ebarb, and five unidentified. (Courtesy of Karen Montgomery.)

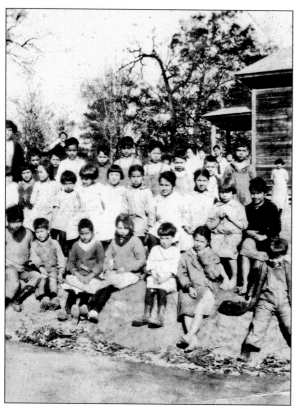

Pictured is teacher Dora Greer's Ebarb class of 1924–1925 at the old "weathertight" school. The students remain largely unidentified but present an interesting picture of what the school and school population looked like at that time. This building is the third Ebarb School. It began as a one-room schoolhouse with an additional room added later. (Courtesy of Marie Polk.)

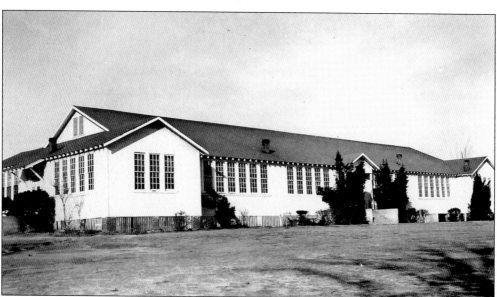

Ebarb High School consisted of first grade through high school. This fourth schoolhouse provided education for several generations of students. It had high ceilings, was not air-conditioned, had wooden floors, and had no screens on the windows. This old building was replaced by a modern structure in 1987, when it was torn down, and remains only in memories and photographs. (Courtesy of Travis Ebarb Jr.)

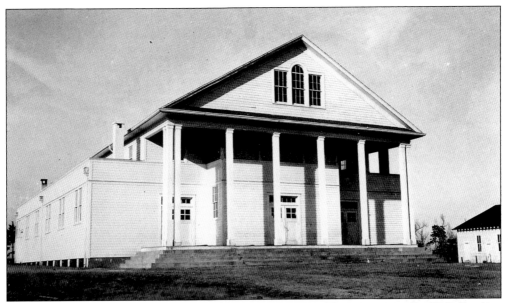

This picture of the Ebarb gymnasium holds many memories. Tournaments or basketball games with Zwolle always ensured a full house as the Ebarb community has always supported the Ebarb Rebels. Ebarb won runner-up in Class C finals in 1969 and was state champion in 1970. Plans are being made to replace it with a more modern building. (Courtesy of Travis Ebarb Jr.)

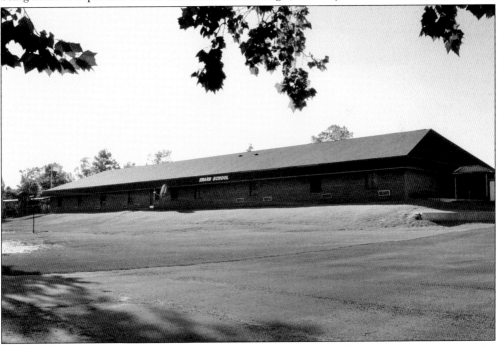

In 1987, a new modern school was built to replace the 1926 schoolhouse that consolidated the Ebarb, Sepulvado, Blue Lake, and Alwood Schools. J. H. Ezernack was the main carpenter who had built the previous schoolhouse. When it needed major repairs, the school board decided a new school was required. This new structure has all modern equipment, including computer lab, science lab, and library. (Courtesy of Martin Crooks.)

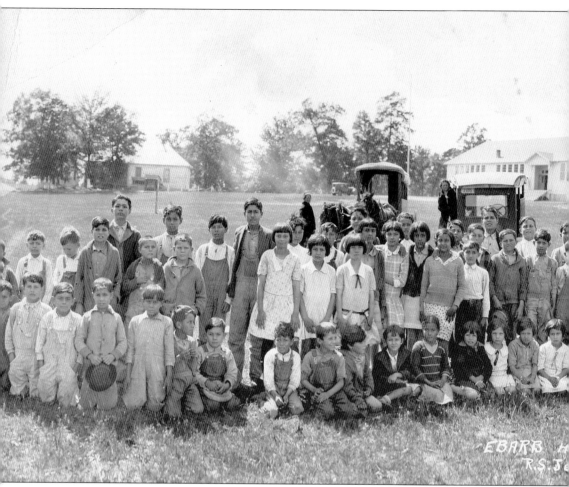

Ebarb High School posed for a picture in 1929 when R. S. Jeansonne was principal. As it took place 77 years ago, even the small children would be in their 80s today. Students and school personnel from left to right are: (first row, kneeling or sitting) three unidentified, Gene Nigreville, six unidentified, Catherine Sepulvado, unidentified, Ethel Sepulvado, Mary Louise Ebarb, unidentified, Addy Sepulvado, Minnie Ebarb, four unidentified, Evelina Ebarb, two unidentified, Ruby Sepulvado, two unidentified, Melva Vines, Myrtie Sepulvado, Evelyn Ebarb, Elvie Garcie, unidentified, Addie Sepulvado, and unidentified; (second row) unidentified, Jimmy Emanus, unidentified, Jessie Ebarb, unidentified, John Ebarb, Sally Ebarb, Lanez Sepulvado, Janie Ebarb, three unidentified, Barbara Procell, Paul H. Sepulvado, three unidentified, Jake Procell, unidentified, Joe William

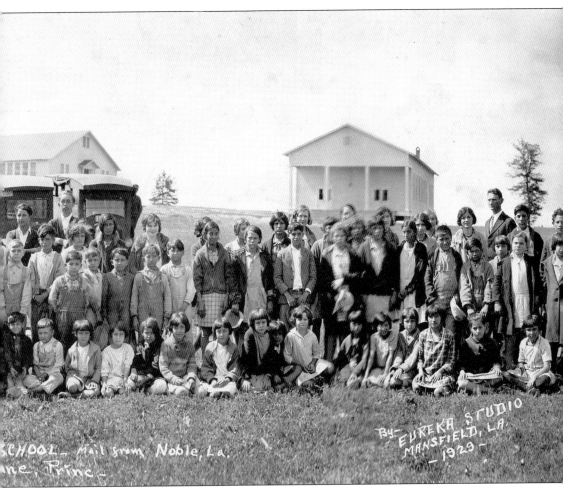

Procell, unidentified, Elmer Procell, unidentified, J. W. Moore, Sam A. Rivers, Beatrice Garcie, ? Everett, unidentified, Myrtle Everett, two unidentified, Paul Henry Ebarb, Wilford Sepulvado, Inez Willis, and two unidentified; (third row) unidentified, Virgil Procell, unidentified, ? Knight, seven unidentified, Henry Knight, two unidentified, Loran Ebarb, Willy Crnkovic, Lenora Procell, three unidentified, Erlene Garcie, Edna Laroux, Mary Criswell, four unidentified, Reba Parrot, two unidentified, Tom Wiley, John Emanus, and Johnny Meshell. Apologies are made for any inaccuracies; after 77 years, there are few people who can identify everyone with 100 percent accuracy. (Courtesy of Marie Polk.)

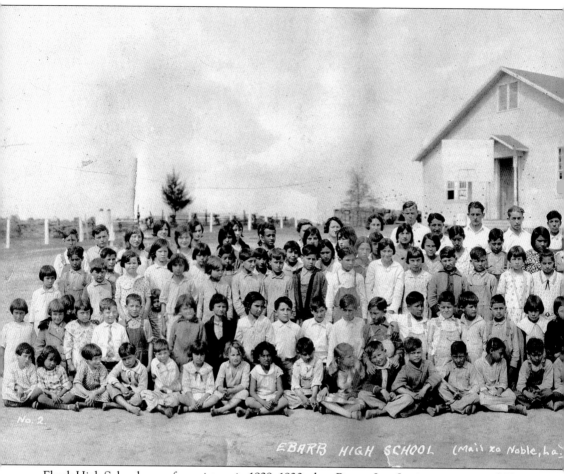

No. 2.

EBARB HIGH SCHOOL (Mail zo Noble, La.)

Ebarb High School poses for a picture in 1929–1930 when Rupert Law Lucius was principal. From Elvera Procell, important facts about Ebarb School are learned. The school consisted of eight rooms and had 110 students and 6 teachers. Four rooms were added to this 8-room building to make a total of 12 rooms. William Ebarb donated one acre of land in 1904 upon which a one-room log cabin was built that housed 30 students and one teacher. The next school was a one-room, standing-plank school, followed by a one-room "weathertight" building, which later had another

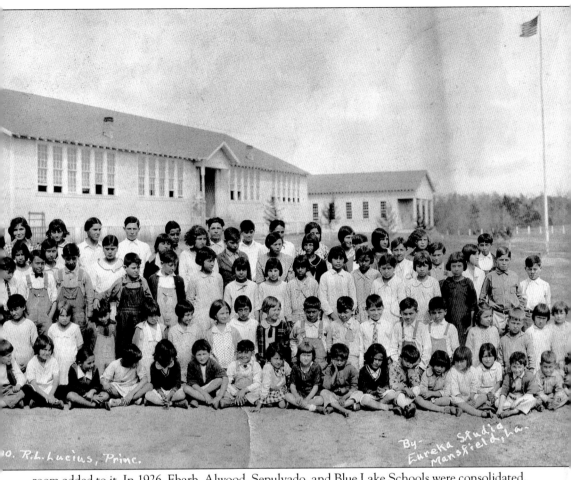

0. R.L. Lucius, Princ.

By-
Eureka Studio
Mansfield, La.

room added to it. In 1926, Ebarb, Alwood, Sepulvado, and Blue Lake Schools were consolidated. This building remained in existence until 1987, when it was replaced by a more modern structure that better serves the education process. In 2006, Ebarb School had an enrollment of 365 students from pre-kindergarten and kindergarten through high school. Victor Sepulvado serves as principal, and 29 teachers are employed at the school. (Courtesy of Marie Polk.)

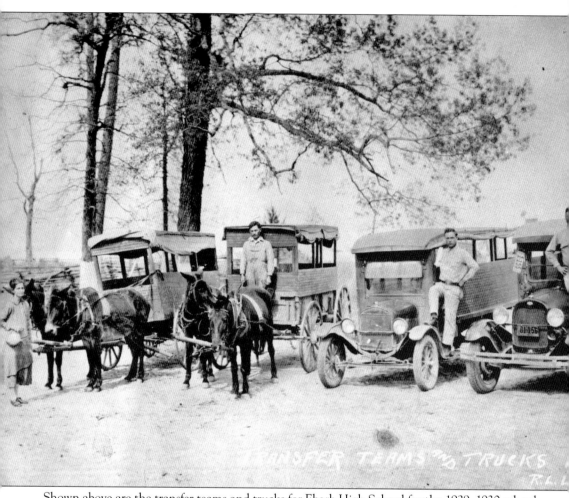

Shown above are the transfer teams and trucks for Ebarb High School for the 1929–1930 school year. Standing next to the mule-drawn vehicles, from left to right, are Mattie Weathy and Henry Chay Procell. Standing on their engine-powered vehicles from left to right are Bud Vines, Jeff Sepulvado, and Frank Garcie. To the right of the five vehicles from left to right are Hattie Procell, Emma (Procell) Rivers holding Leo, Nora Procell, Nancy Procell, Sally Pipps, Foster Paddie, Lena

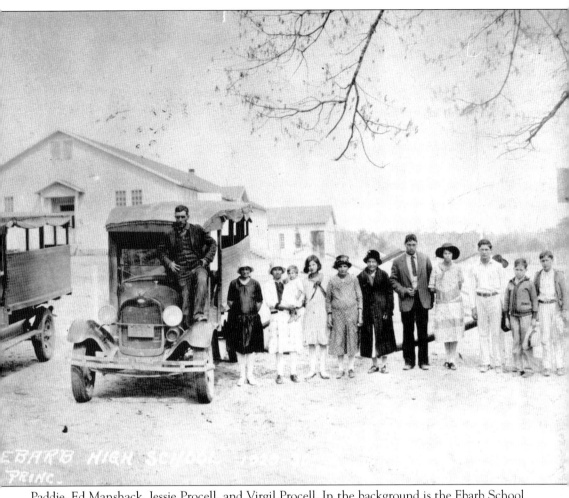

EBARB HIGH SCHOOL
PRINC.

Paddie, Ed Manshack, Jessie Procell, and Virgil Procell. In the background is the Ebarb School Complex. Getting to and from school could be time consuming, dangerous, and expensive. Oftentimes the drivers would remain at school until dismissal. They took food for themselves and their animals. Roads were unpaved, and they sometimes flooded or washed out. Getting up the Eli Garcie Hill was quite a challenge. (Courtesy of Raymond L. and Joan Ebarb.)

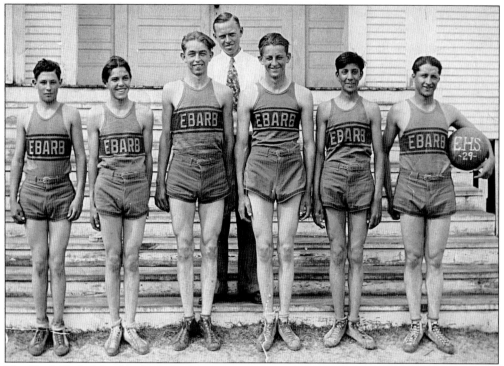

The Ebarb High School basketball team in 1929 is shown with principal Rupert Law Lucius. Sports as well as academics have always played an important part of life around Ebarb. Pictured from left to right are Wilson Leone, George Weathy, William Crnkovic, Rudolph Crnkovic, John W. Emanus, and Loran Ebarb. Loran later became a teacher and principal at Ebarb where he was to spend 30 years of his professional life. (Courtesy of John C. and Carla Ebarb.)

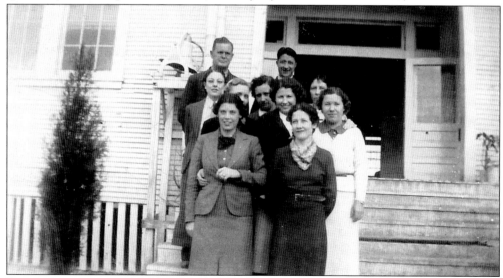

Principal A. A. Key and the faculty pose for a picture in the 1937–1938 school year. From left to right are (first row) Madge Ellzey and Ethel Holiday; (second row) Corine McCartney, Reba Hardin Parrot, Elvera Martinez Ebarb Procell, Lula Mae Longoria, Eva Laroux Ebarb, and Lucille Klotz Ebarb; (third row) A. A. Key and Loran Ebarb. (Courtesy of Marie Polk.)

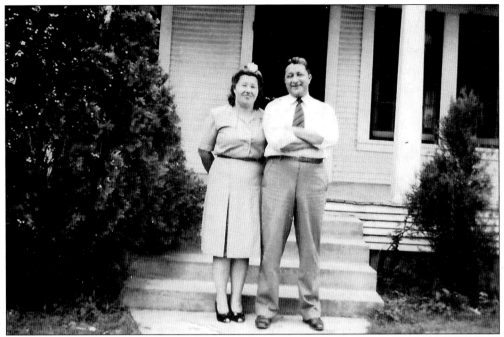

Lucille Klotz and Loran Ebarb pose in front of the Home Economics Building in the 1940s. Ebarb began as a teacher at Ebarb and later became principal. Klotz was originally from Iowa but had gone to school at Northwestern State College. She was the home economics teacher for many years. (Courtesy of Marie Polk.)

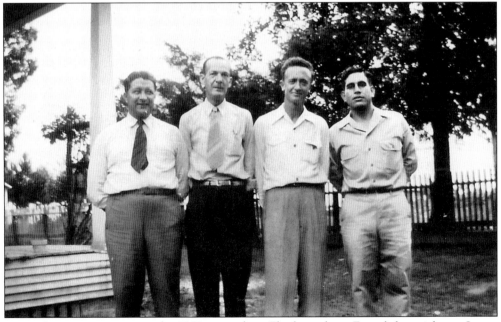

Posing for a group picture in the 1940s were these Ebarb teachers. From left to right are Loran Ebarb, W. D. Kimbrell, Luther Harvey, and Floyd Lopez. All were deceased by 2006 except Floyd Lopez, who still lives in Many and is 86 years old. Ebarb was the only one of the group who remained at Ebarb School as principal. (Courtesy of Marie Polk.)

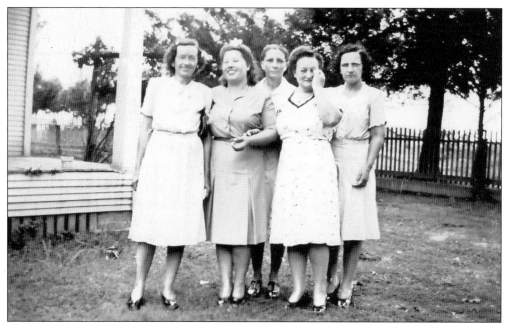

Posing by the Home Economics Building are these teachers. From left to right are Irene Cates, Lucille Klotz Ebarb, Eva Laroux Ebarb, Irene Ross, and Elvera Martinez Ebarb Procell. Notice the picket fence to keep out stray animals. "Granny" glasses and shoes have made a comeback and are stylish again. (Courtesy of Marie Polk.)

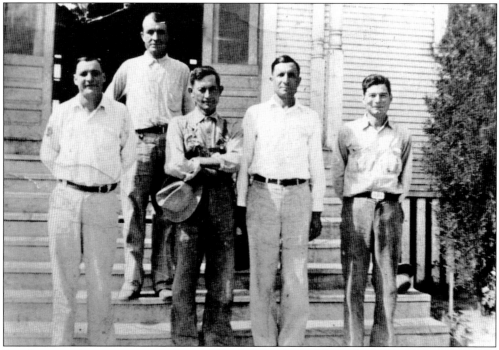

Bus drivers and a janitor pose in front of Ebarb School, possibly in the 1930s. From left to right are Lee Meshell, janitor George Sepulvado, Henry Chay Procell, Dora Sepulvado, and David Rivers. (Courtesy of Margie Rivers.)

Ebarb's first-team basketball team in 1937 from left to right was (first row) Catherine Sepulvado, Janie Sepulvado, and Margie Sepulvado; (second row) Mary Louise Ebarb and Bertha Rivers; (third row) Ruby Sepulvado, Mary Ann Leone, and Grace Rivers. The girls' basketball team was discontinued for a while and reinstituted in the 1970s. (Courtesy of Muriel Rivers.)

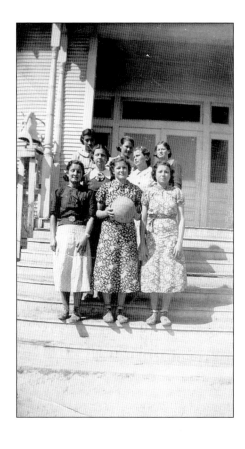

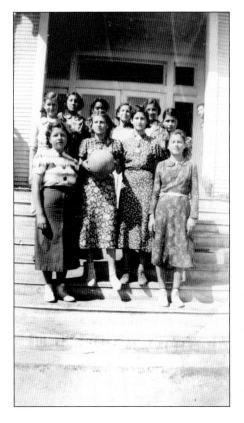

The members of the second team at Ebarb School in 1937 from left to right were (first row) Gladys Bebee, Rosell Garcie (holding the basketball), Mary Addie Sepulvado, and Bertie Sepulvado; (second row) Cecil Ebarb, Mertis Sepulvado, Beatrice Garcie, Lavell Garcie, Verna Sepulvado, and Artie Mae Ebarb. (Courtesy of Pauline Ebarb.)

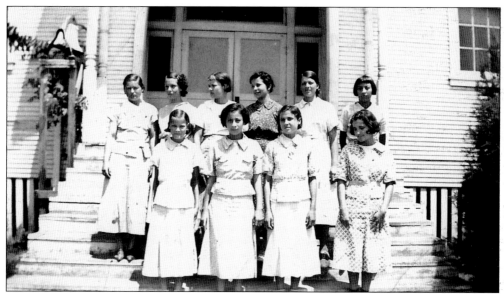

Posing for a group picture was this class of Ebarb students. From left to right are (first row) Minnie Ebarb, Evelyn Ebarb, Margie Sepulvado, and Catherine Sepulvado; (second row) Grace Rivers, Mary Louise Ebarb, Dorothy Mora, Lanez Sepulvado, Minnie Sepulvado, and Ruby Sepulvado. (Courtesy of Marie Polk.)

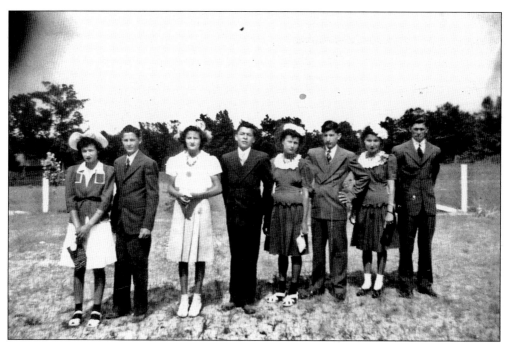

Ebarb students pose for a picture. From left to right are Christell Sepulvado, Tony Ebarb, Mable Sepulvado, Bert Sepulvado, Verna Procell, Martin Sepulvado, Virgie Procell, and Herman Ebarb. It was possibly the late 1930s or early 1940s when this picture was taken. (Courtesy of Pauline Ebarb.)

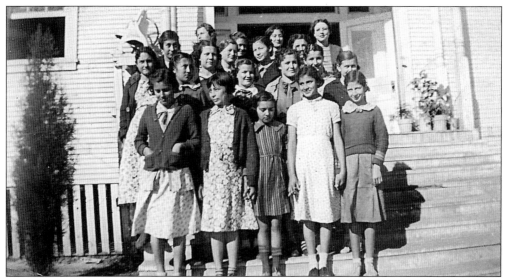

Teacher Corrine McCartney and her class pose for a picture. From left to right are (first row) Bertie Sepulvado, Pauline Ebarb, Marie Ebarb, Verna Sepulvado, and Lovell Garcie; (second row) Bertie Mae Sepulvado, Myrtie Sepulvado, Minnie Ebarb, Janie Sepulvado, Catherine Sepulvado, and Cecil Ebarb; (third row) Ruby Sepulvado, Mary Louise Ebarb, Grace Rivers, Evelyn Ebarb, and Margie Sepulvado; (fourth row) Bertha Rivers, Mary Ann Leone, and Addie Sepulvado. (Courtesy of Pauline Ebarb.)

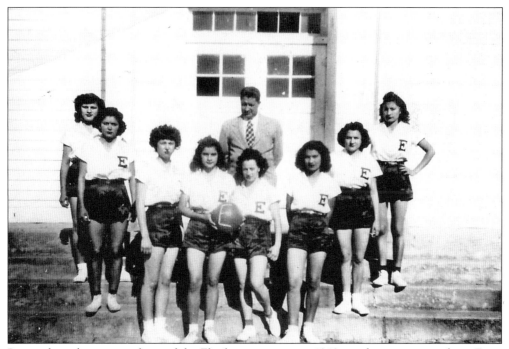

Pictured on the steps in front of the Ebarb gymnasium in 1948 are these team members. From left to right are Aline Mora, Alice Ebarb, Nola Sepulvado, Iva Lee Ebarb, Hester Ebarb, Roberta Manshack, Elaine Sepulvado, and Della Sepulvado. In the background is principal Loran Ebarb. (Courtesy of Marie Polk.)

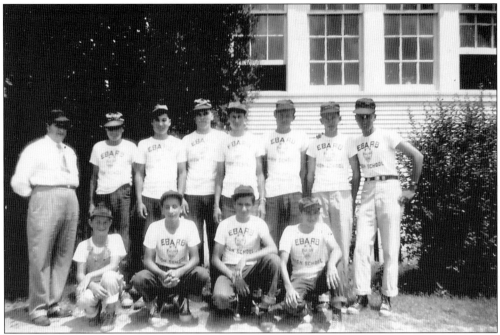

The boys' baseball team, about 1948–1949, poses in front of the school. From left to right are (first row) Merle Jean Lewis, Pat Ebarb, Max Sepulvado, and Simon Sepulvado; (second row) Principal Loran Ebarb, John C. Ebarb, Carson Rivers, Junior Procell, Herman R. Sepulvado, E. C. Vines, James Roland Ebarb, and Sammy Bruce Procell. (Courtesy of Marie Polk.)

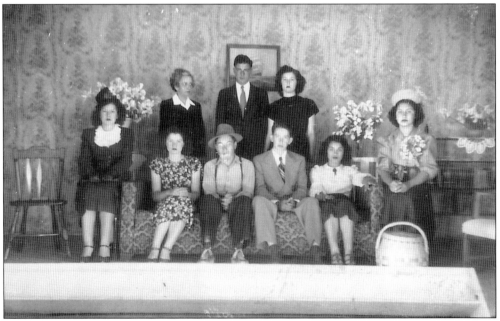

On March 22, 1949, the Ebarb senior class presented their play, the *Absent Minded Professor*, in the Ebarb gymnasium. Cast members were, from left to right, (seated) Rosa Lee Sepulvado, Hazel Sepulvado, Max Sepulvado, James Roland Ebarb, Roberta Manshack, and Della Sepulvado; (standing) Iva Lee Ebarb, Sammy Bruce Procell, and Anola Sepulvado. (Courtesy of Marie Polk.)

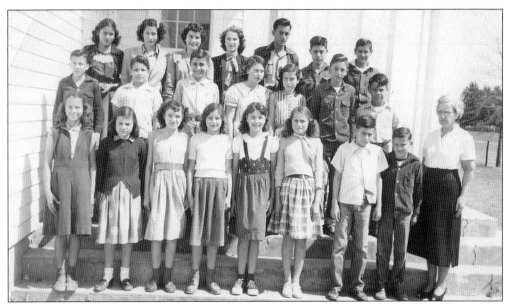

Pictured is teacher Elvera Procell's class. From left to right are (first row) Thelma Rivers, Helen Ebarb, Vernita Meshell, Louise Sepulvado, Shawnee Sepulvado, Lenez Mora, J. W. Sepulvado, Travis Ebarb, and teacher Elvera Procell; (second row) Sammie Garcie, Perkins Sepulvado, Jimmy Meshell, Carolyn Ebarb, Eloise Garcie, Nick Manshack, and Randolph Ebarb; (third row) Juanna Procell, Dorothy Etheridge, Ethel Ebarb, Jeanie Martinez, Billy Ray Laroux, Charles Laroux, and Marvin Sepulvado. (Courtesy of Marie Polk.)

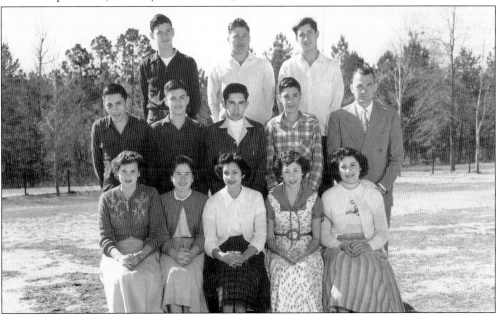

The sophomore class of 1954–1955 is shown posing for a class picture. From left to right are (first row) Belva Jean Meshell, Doris Faye Rivers, Ruth Sepulvado, Mary Jane Garcie, and Joan Ebarb; (second row) Charles Sepulvado, Louis Procell, Jimmy Ray Sepulvado, Hosea Eugene Sepulvado, and teacher Rogers Loupe; (third row) Raymond Procell, John Earl Rivers, and Gabe Mora. (Courtesy of Marie Polk.)

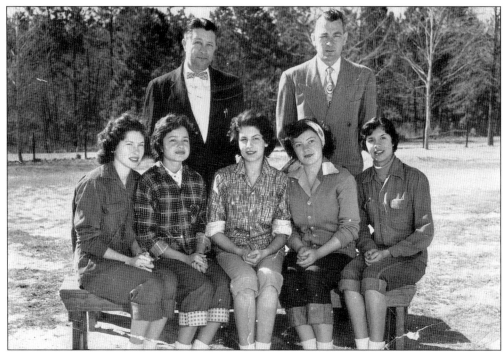

Looking spiffy in their 1950s outfits are, from left to right, (seated) Catherine Ebarb, Shirley Ebarb, Lula Mae Sepulvado, Bernadette Procell, and Mary Hildred Procell; (standing) principal Loran Ebarb and teacher Rogers Loupe. Rolled-up jeans, white socks, penny loafers, and oxfords were the latest rage. (Courtesy of Judy Ebarb.)

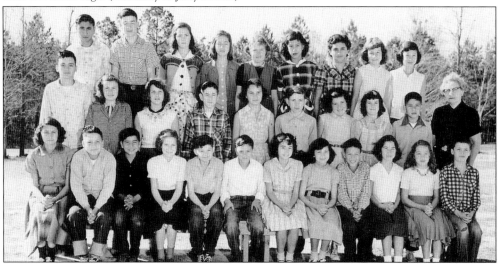

Pictured is teacher Elvera Procell's class. From left to right are (first row) Pearl Malmay, Amos Parrie, Paul Sepulvado, Lizzie Etheridge, Wayne Ebarb, Willis Sepulvado, Ella Garcie, Agatha Sepulvado, David Garcie, Emma Rivers, Rose Ebarb, and Sammy Rivers; (second row) Julius Sepulvado, Alice Sepulvado, Theresa Meshell, Leon Sepulvado, Janie Ebarb, Arthur Mora, Faye Procell, Arvell Lee, Burlin Procell, and teacher Elvera Procell; (third row) Maurice Malmay, Ed Sepulvado, Loree Ezernack, Lorena Sepulvado, Sybil Ebarb, Shirley Malmay, Edith Sepulvado, Loretta Procell, and Rita Rivers. (Courtesy of Marie Polk.)

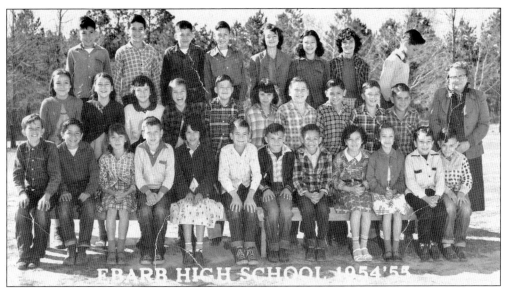

Pictured is teacher ? Mims's class. From left to right are (first row) Wallace Lee, Kenneth Ebarb, Evelyn Tate, Sammy Meshell, Elizabeth Ebarb, Manuel Sepulvado, Chester Meshell, A. J. Malmay, Joyce Garcie, Elsie Ebarb, Joe Ebarb, and Chris Sepulvado; (second row) Shirley Sepulvado, Magaline Rivers, Edith Ebarb, Rosemary Procell, Danna Procell, Mary Sepulvado, Ben Rivers, Leroy Sepulvado, Benny Sepulvado, Curtis Ebarb, and teacher ? Mims; (third row) William Laroux, Steve Ebarb, Anthony Sepulvado, Harvey Sepulvado, Mildred Sepulvado, Edell Sepulvado, Margie Campbell, and Tom Ebarb. (Courtesy of Sue Ellen [Laroux] Remedies.)

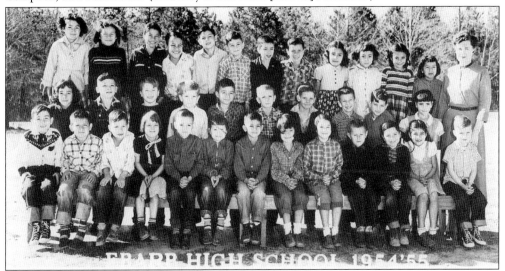

Pictured is teacher Irma McComic's class. From left to right are (first row) Russell Tyner, Howard Ebarb, Sammy Procell, Patricia Rivers, J. W. Malmay, Anna Rivers, Tommy Sepulvado, Cecilia Ebarb, Faye Ebarb, George Dunn, J. P. Ebarb, Thelma Brown, and Vernon Ebarb; (second row) Christell Laroux, Clarence Malmay, Jimmy Rivers, Glen Sepulvado, Clayton Sepulvado, Alfred Sepulvado, Roger Sharbeno, Herbert Ebarb, Terry Ebarb, Myrtle Campbell, and teacher Irma McComic; (third row) Clara Procell, Linda Procell, Monroe Mora, Glen Ebarb, unidentified, Roy Garcie, Eddie Logan, Arvis Lee, Jeanine Ebarb, Bernice Malmay, Virginia Garcie, and Margie Sepulvado. (Courtesy of Terry Ebarb.)

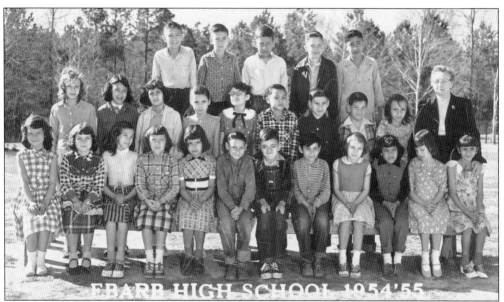

Pictured is teacher Irene Ross's class. From left to right are (first row) Dorothy Faye Procell, Trudie Lee, Lucille Procell, Joyce Ann Sepulvado, Barbara Laroux, William Ernest Sepulvado, Howard Laroux, Clarence Procell, Sue Ebarb, Marie Laroux, Bonnie Marie Leone, and Mildred Malmay; (second row) Bertha Sepulvado, Yvonne Leone, Theresa Sepulvado, Lurline Castillo, Dorothy Malmay, Jessie Castillo, Gary Sepulvado, Sam Rivers Jr., Shirley Sepulvado, and teacher Irene Ross; (third row) David Meshell, Clifton Sepulvado, Hugh Procell, Carroll Sepulvado, and Duce Malmay. (Courtesy of Sue Ellen [Laroux] Remedies.)

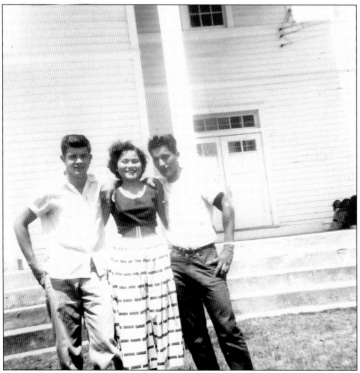

Smiling for the picture in front of the Ebarb gymnasium are DeWitt Meshell (left), Thelma Castillo (center), and Sonny Manshack. This photograph was taken in 1955. The world was getting ready for Elvis Presley to appear on the musical scene. (Courtesy of Joe Ebarb.)

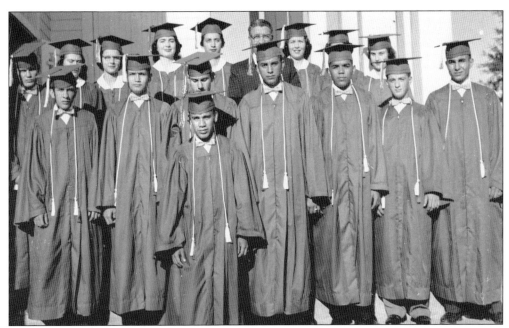

This is a picture of the Ebarb High School senior class of 1959–1960. From left to right are (front, center) Marvin Randolph Ebarb; (first row) Sammie Joseph Garcie, Perkins Sepulvado, James Wilson Sepulvado, Nick Manshack, Pete Parrie, Robert Dale Leone, and Jimmie Ray Meshell; (second row) Richard Travis Ebarb, Carolyn Ruth Ebarb, Mary Louise Sepulvado, Aline Ebarb, Mary Helen Sepulvado, Loran Ebarb, Shawnee Sepulvado, Dorothy Ethridge, and Elouise Dolores Garcie. (Courtesy of Marie Polk.)

Some of the Ebarb seniors are, from left to right, (first row) Johnny Sepulvado, Annette Laroux, and Mildred Sepulvado; (second row) George Garcie and Rupert Sepulvado. This picture was taken at St. Joseph's Church in Zwolle, probably at graduation ceremonies honoring that year's graduates. (Courtesy of Sue Ellen [Laroux] Remedies.)

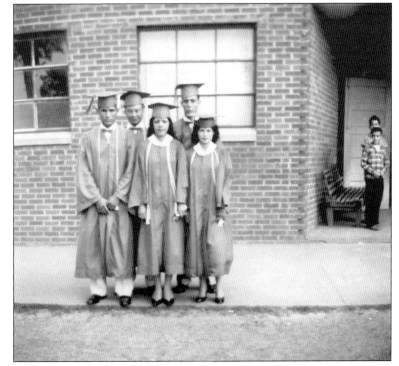

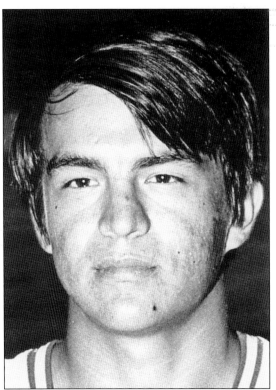

Greg Procell, a product of Ebarb High School in Sabine Parish, was a scoring machine. He is the nation's all-time basketball top scorer, scoring 6,702 points—a 37.2-point per-game average in his four years at Ebarb High School. He set a state single-game scoring record of 100 points in 1970 (there were no three pointers then). He was inducted into the Louisiana Sports Hall of Fame in 1988, the only athlete ever to make it primarily on his prep career. (Courtesy of Louisiana Sports Hall of Fame.)

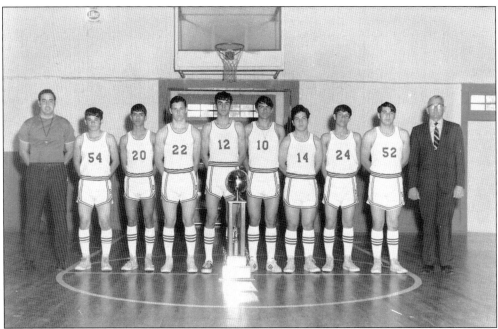

Ebarb High School's basketball team is pictured. They were the 1970 Class C Champions. From left to right are Coach Ken Hebert, Bernis Sepulvado, Donald Lester Sepulvado, Junior Kirk, Walter Meshell Jr., Greg Procell, Julius Ebarb, Frank Procell, Roger Rivers, and principal Rogers Loupe. (Courtesy of Travis Ebarb Jr.)

Five

FORESTRY AND LOGGING INDUSTRY

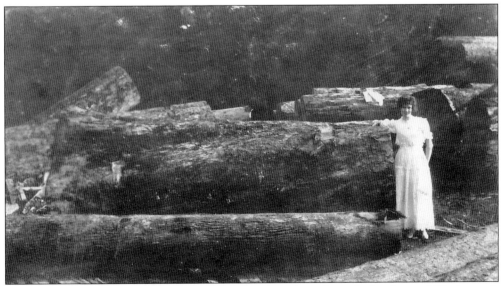

Bessie Gaul stands beside some huge logs that have been brought to the lumberyard. Timberwork could be slow, tedious, and dangerous. Bessie's brothers and sisters were Katie, Mae, Tom, and William. The Gaul family operated a hotel that provided room and board for those needing their services. This photograph was taken in either the late 1920s or early 1930s. (Courtesy of the Roy Procell collection.)

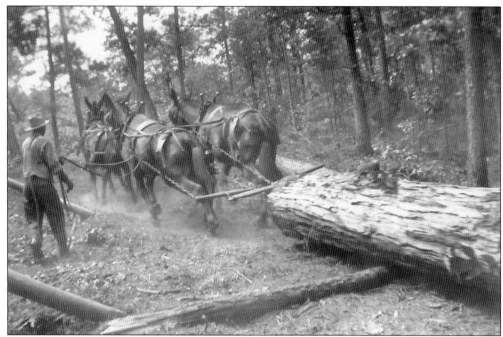

Loggers used teams of horses, mules, or oxen to skid (pull, drag, or haul) the logs to a landing in a central place in the woods. Some trees were very large, and it was quite a feat to decide what was the most efficient way to get them moved to the loading places. (Courtesy of Wanda Sepulvado.)

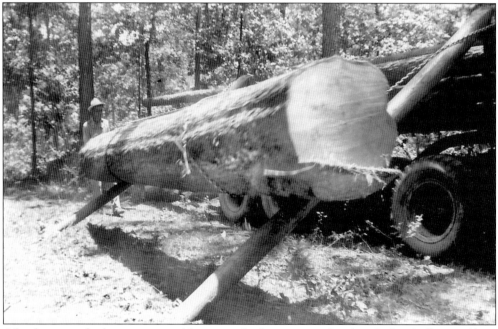

After bringing the logs to a central location, the loggers were faced with the challenge of how to safely get these huge logs onto wagons, trams, and later trucks. Using poles, chains, animals, and a good dose of ingenuity, they managed to load, chain, and fasten them properly. (Courtesy of Wanda Sepulvado.)

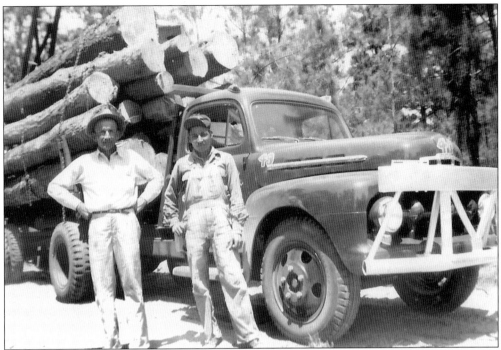

This picture shows workers standing by their loaded log truck. From left to right are Herman Martinez and Jefferson Cesar (J. C.) Sepulvado. Taken in 1950, the men were hauling logs for Mansfield Hardwood Lumber Company, in Zwolle. The timber industry has become more mechanized, and the trucks are more streamlined and energy efficient. (Courtesy of Wanda Sepulvado.)

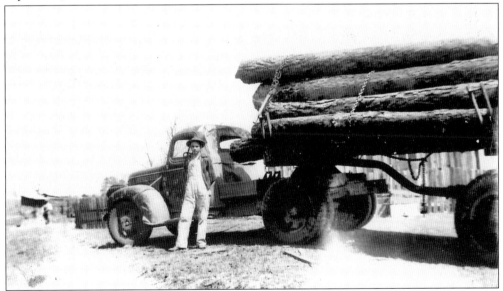

Freddie Louis Craig poses beside his log truck. Trucks in the 1940s and 1950s were not as sophisticated as they are today. Trucks would break down and were quite dangerous. Freddie's sons are Jackie, Michael, Ricky Lee, and Danny Wayne. His stepsons are George Henderson, Donald Henderson, and K. G. Henderson. (Courtesy of Cody Bruce.)

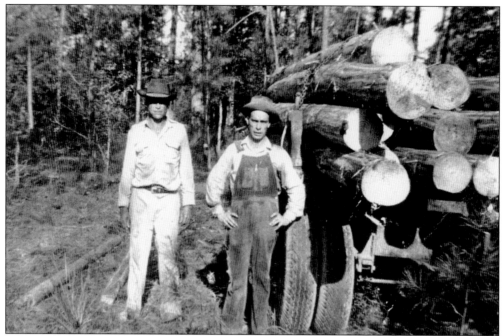

Martin Santos (left) and Jessie Procell are shown posing for a picture beside their loaded log truck. Most men in Sabine Parish in the 1950s and 1960s made their living from the timber industry. Interestingly enough, even in 2006, timber is a huge industry in Northwest Louisiana. (Courtesy of Curtis Sepulvado.)

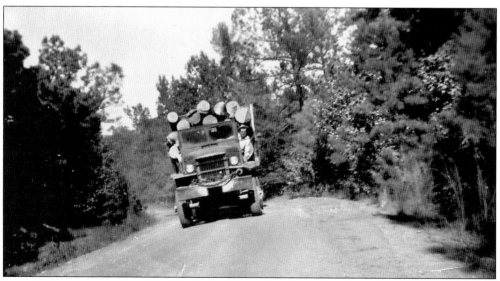

James Bebee peers out the side of his loaded log truck as he makes his way to a local sawmill. He worked many years in this industry in both Leesville and Sabine Parish. His wife was Helen (Burson) Bebee. Their children are Joan, Elaine, Patsy, and Gayla. (Courtesy of Wanda Sepulvado.)

Six

TOLEDO BEND, OUR HERITAGE, AND FESTIVALS

Roy Rogers, famed "King of the Cowboys" and singing and western movie star of the 1940s and 1950s, visited Toledo Bend. This picture was taken in October 1969. Shown from left to right are Lee Bryant, owner of Channel 6 Studios in Shreveport, Louisiana; Roy Rogers; Jim Clark, champion pistol shooter; and Charlie Anderson, manager of Anderson's Camp. This story was printed in the *Sabine News*, a local newspaper in Zwolle, whose editor was Roy Procell. (Courtesy of Archie Lee Anderson.)

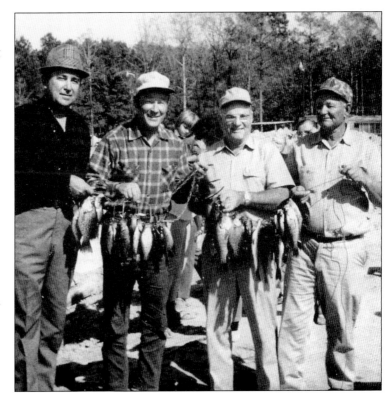

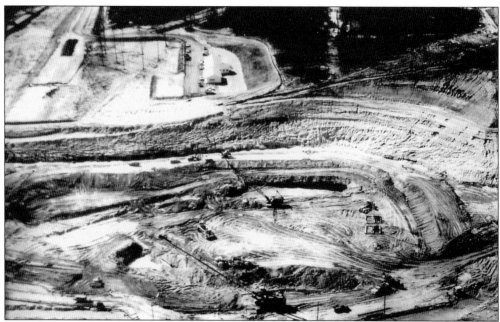

In 1949, Texas created the Sabine River Authority of Texas. The following year, Louisiana created the Sabine River Authority of Louisiana. The two respective states were charged with conserving and developing the waters of the Sabine River for beneficial purposes. After a feasibility study in 1959, Texas and Louisiana arranged for the financing of $30 million in hydroelectric revenue bonds. Land acquisition began in May 1963, and construction of the dam, spillway, and power plant was initiated in April 1964. The closure section of the earthen embankment and impoundment of water was begun in October 1966. The power plant was completed and began operating in the early part of 1969. (Courtesy of Frank Dutton/Toledo-Bend.us and Toledo-Bend.com.)

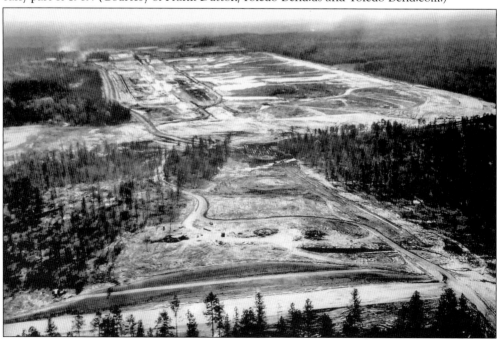

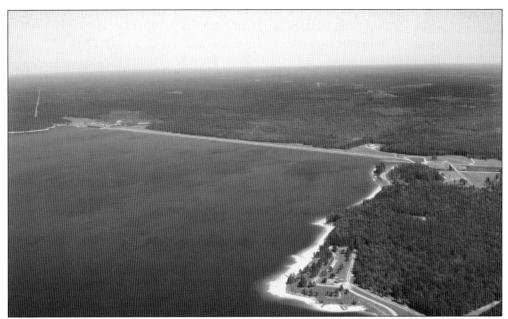

The Toledo Bend Lake area is composed of over 185,000 acres. It is the largest man-made body of water in the South and the fifth largest in surface in the United States. Its 1,200 miles of shoreline offer almost unlimited opportunity for both private and public recreational development. The lake is 65 miles long with only one bridge spanning its width. The three-mile-long Pendleton Bridge is approximately midway down the length of the reservoir. The reservoir is famous for its excellent fishing and is rated one of the top five bass lakes in the nation. Largemouth bass, crappie, bream, catfish, and striper bass are also plentiful. Water sports enthusiasts also enjoy swimming, boating, sailing, Jet Skiing, canoeing, and SCUBA diving. (Courtesy of Frank Dutton/Toledo-Bend.us and Toledo-Bend.com.)

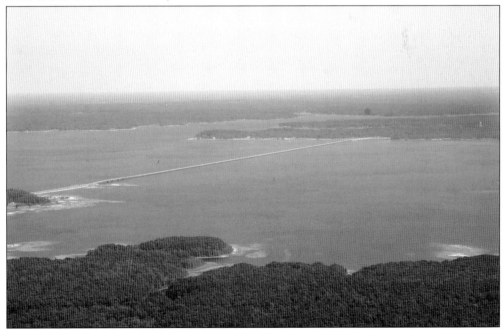

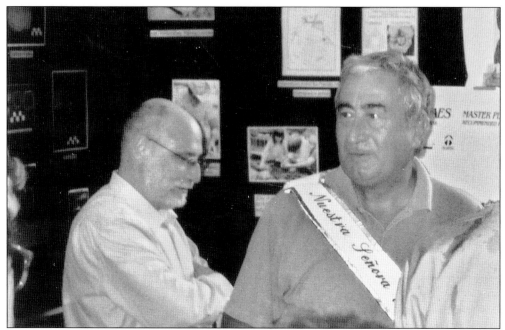

The Spanish Duke of San Carlos (right), who visited the Los Adaes State Historic Site in fall 2003, is the highest-ranking Spanish official to visit this site. Also in the picture on the left is an unidentified Spanish interpreter. Los Adaes was the capital of Texas from 1721 until the Spanish were forced to abandon East Texas in 1773. (Courtesy of Los Adaes State Historic Site/Office of Louisiana State Parks.)

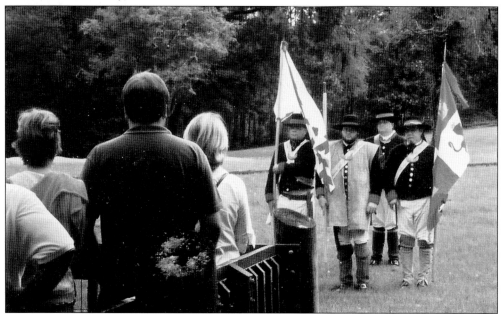

During the visit of the Duke of San Carlos, Los Adaes staff members and volunteers portrayed Spanish Colonial soldiers at Los Adaes State Historic Park. The Soldado Honor Guard is, from left to right, Mark Ayres, Jared Dodd, Randy Jessie Smith Jr., and Corneal Cox. (Courtesy of Los Adaes State Historic Site/Office of Louisiana State Parks.)

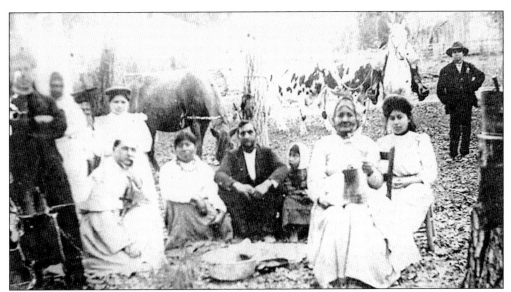

In the early 1900s, Father Van Haver (far left) and another priest, possibly a Carmelite because of his white habit and large cross, pose with the Toby family of 100-percent Choctaw descent. The family attended a mission at the church during which time they would camp beside the church. Present were Louisa Toby Procella, Hosea Procella, Mary Procella, Martha Toby Carmona, and Dora Toby Garza. (Courtesy of Ernest Rodrigues and Cody Bruce.)

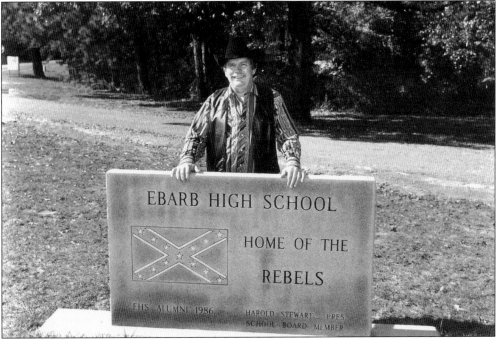

Raymond L. Ebarb, a direct descendant of Antonio Gil Y'Barbo, poses in front of the Ebarb School monument. He is the son of Emmett and Eva (Laroux) Ebarb. He came back to Ebarb to teach agriculture after he finished his education. He married Joan Emanus, and they have one son, Pedro. Raymond was the first chief of the Choctaw-Apache Tribe of Ebarb. (Courtesy of Raymond L. and Joan Ebarb.)

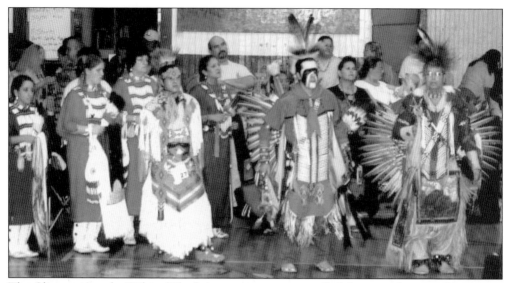

The Choctaw-Apache Tribe of Ebarb is participating in a tribal dance at the annual pow-wow that took place in the Ebarb gymnasium. Often it was held outside in the ballpark. In 2006, it took place at the Zwolle Festival grounds. These pow-wows are important events because they serve as a means of maintaining friendships and sharing news and information. (Courtesy of Frank Dutton/Toledo-Bend.us and Toledo-Bend.com.)

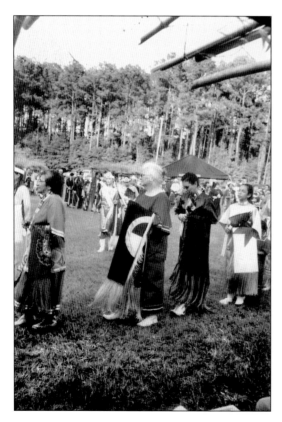

This picture was taken during the ceremonies at the Choctaw-Apache Annual Tradition Pow-Wow. From left to right are chief volunteer at tribal office Virginia Malmay, Lisa D. Malmay, and Tory B. Parrie. Each year, the Choctaw-Apache group celebrates their connections to tradition and spirituality, to the Earth, and to one another in a social, personal, and spiritual meeting: the pow-wow. (Courtesy of Virginia Malmay.)

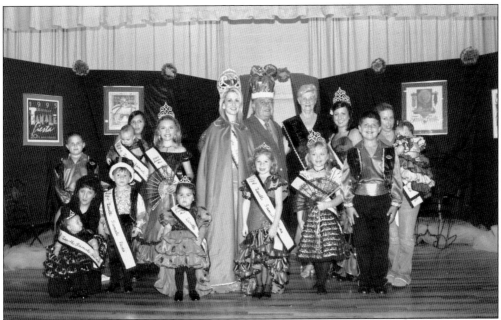

Shown is the 2005 Fiesta Court with the Tamale Fiesta King Bill Leone and Queen Markay Martinez. First Lady of the Fiesta was Lady Patton, who has helped with the pageant for many years. The fiesta celebrates the Spanish and Native American heritage of Northwest Louisiana. (Courtesy of Martin Crooks.)

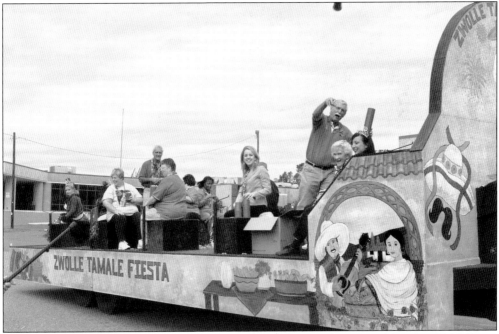

The Zwolle Tamale Fiesta Float makes its way down the parade route in October 2005. Fiesta president Chris Loupe throws cups to parade goers. Chris is the son of Rogers Loupe, who is one of the founders of the Tamale Fiesta. His mother is Ruth (Ebarb) Loupe, a descendant of Antonio Gil Y'Barbo. (Courtesy of Martin Crooks.)

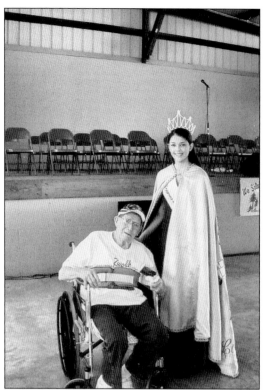

Jim Phillips had the honor of being the "Oldest Logger" at the Loggers Festival in 2006; the queen was Haley Mitchell. The Zwolle Loggers and Forestry celebration is held each year during the second weekend in May. It commemorates the area's relationship with the timber industry and how it has been an industrial base for the entire region. (Courtesy of Wanda Ezernack.)

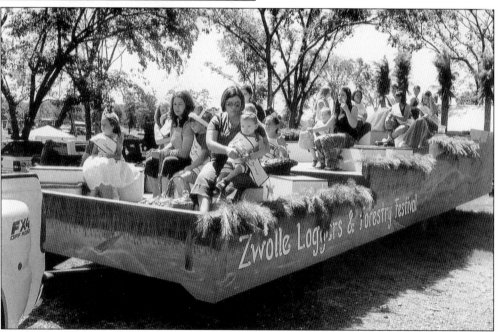

The Loggers' float during the festival parade included festival royalty. This parade takes place on Saturday morning before the day's festivities begin. Included in the parade are log trucks and other equipment that loggers use in the present. Other activities scheduled include a log weight guessing contest, a carnival, street dance, and loading contest. (Courtesy of Wanda Ezernack.)

Seven

OUR FAMILY NAMES

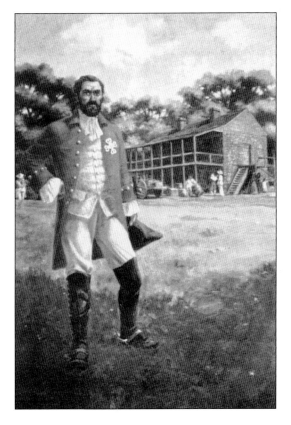

Antonio Gil Y'Barbo (1729–1809), from whom many present-day occupants of Ebarb can trace their direct lineage, was born at Fort Los Adaes. Y'Barbo married Maria Padilla and had four children, Mariano, Marcos, Maria Antonia, and Maria Josefa. He later became lieutenant governor, chief justice, captain of the militia, and founder of modern-day Nacogdoches, Texas. (Courtesy of Nacogdoches Convention and Visitor's Bureau.)

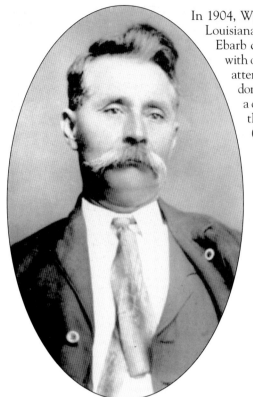

In 1904, William Ebarb rode his horse 17 miles to Many, Louisiana, for the judge's approval to build a school for the Ebarb community. The judge granted him permission with one restriction: there had to be 25 to 30 students to attend the school. Finding more than 30 students, he donated one acre of land. The judge sent a teacher, and a one-room log schoolhouse was built. William was the great-great-grandson of Antonio Gil Y'Barbo. (Courtesy of John C. and Carla Ebarb.)

Stephanie "Fannie" (Nigreville) Ebarb (1854–January 13, 1927), wife of William Ebarb (January 18, 1855–April 2, 1933), was the daughter of Francis Nigreville and Marie Laroux. William is the son of Alcario (Y'barbo) Ebarb and Martina (Sharnac) Ezernack. Alcario is thought to be the first person to change the name Y'Barbo to Ebarb. Stephanie and William's children are Mary, Phillip, Jessie, Joseph, Mattie, Cary, William Jr., Juana, Paul, Lucille, Fannie, and Patrick. (Courtesy of Karen Montgomery.)

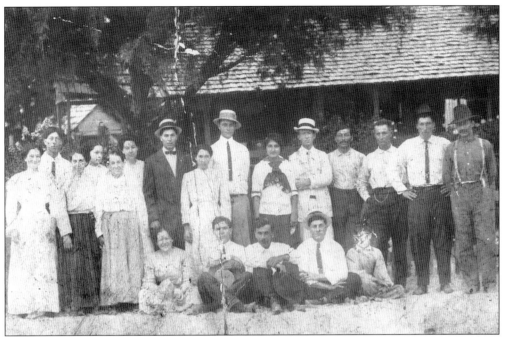

Posing in front of William and Stephanie Ebarb's home were, from left to right, (seated) Lee Hubley, Colon Thames, Tyne Procell, Paul Ebarb, and Pat Ebarb; (standing) Josephine (Ezernack) Ebarb, Cary Ebarb, Mary Mora, Fannie Martinez, Stephanie "Fannie" Ebarb, Mattie (Ebarb) Procell, Bill Ebarb, Lucy Y'Barbo, Sam Ebarb, Maggie Ferguson, ? Pilcher (a teacher), Phillip Ebarb, William Ebarb, Martin Ebarb, and Peter Ebarb. (Courtesy of Marie Polk.)

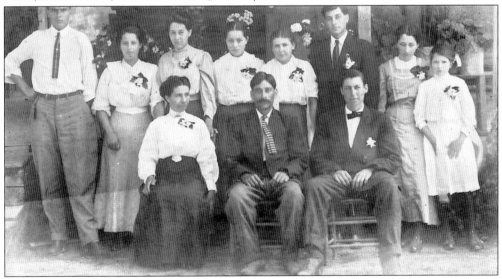

A gathering of the extended Ebarb family in the early 1900s are, from left to right (seated) Mary (Ebarb) Mora, Jessie Ebarb, and Martin Ebarb; (standing) Colon Thames, Rosie (Ebarb) Sepulvado, Mattie (Ebarb) Procell, Fannie (Ebarb) Martinez, Eva Longoria, Paul Ebarb, Lucy (Ebarb) Y'Barbo, and Maggie (Ebarb) Kezerle. Large families were the normal occurrence back then because everyone needed large families to work and help make a living for their extended families. (Courtesy of Marie Polk.)

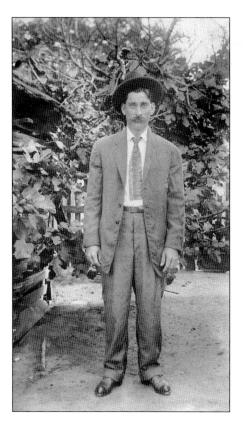

Jessie Ebarb, son of William and Stephanie "Fannie" Nigreville Ebarb, was born on January 14, 1881. A story is told about how he was killed on January 20, 1915, by people stealing the Ebarbs' hogs. He approached these people, who killed him and left him hanging from the stirrups of the horse's saddle. (Courtesy of Marie Polk.)

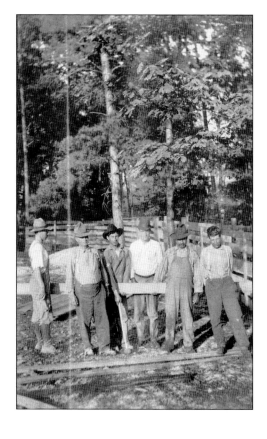

Building a vat for cattle dipping are, from left to right, Pat Ebarb, William Ebarb, Ben Knight, Alex Sepulvado, Tom Ebarb, and Peter Ebarb. Remnants of these old cattle dips can be found at some deserted home places. The vats were used to dip the cattle into creosote to kill insects (ticks, fleas, lice) that tormented the cattle. (Courtesy of Marie Polk.)

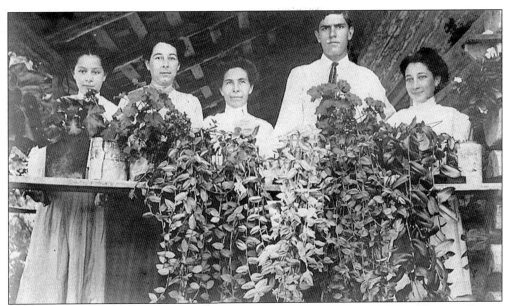

Posing for a picture on the front porch of the Ebarb family home from left to right were Fannie (Ebarb) Martinez, Mattie (Ebarb) Procell, Mary (Ebarb) Mora, Colon Thames, and Lucy (Ebarb) Y'Barbo. Ruth (Ebarb) Loupe and Kathryn (Ebarb) Boudreaux, twin sisters, still have this green thumb; today they have beautiful flower gardens, which include wandering jew or *Tradescantia pallida*. (Courtesy of Marie Polk.)

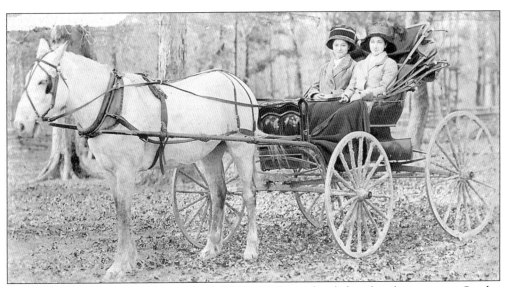

Fanny Ebarb (1897–1977) and Lucy Ebarb (1893–1994) were headed to church on a winter Sunday morning. They are dressed in cold-weather clothing while wearing very chic hats. Really poor people did not own a horse and carriage but were happy to have a horse and wagon. Ebarb was about seven miles from Zwolle, so they probably did not make this trip alone very often. (Courtesy of Ione Durr.)

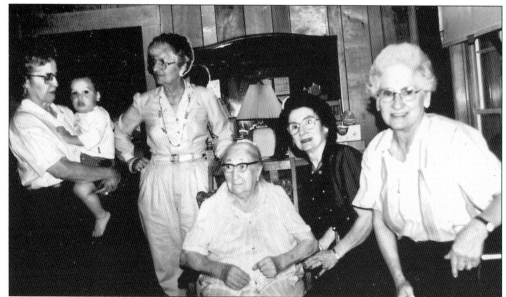

In 1986, Lucy (Ebarb) Y'Barbo celebrated her 93rd birthday. Helping the birthday girl celebrate from left to right are Kathryn (Ebarb) Boudreaux holding Andrew Montgomery, Vivian Ebarb, Lucy (Ebarb) Y'Barbo, Polly Moyer, and Theo (Ebarb) Ezernack. Lucy is buried in the Chireno Catholic Cemetery in Nacogdoches County, Texas. She was married about 1908 to James Ellis Y'Barbo, son of Juan Condy Y'Barbo and Margaret Montes. (Courtesy of Karen Montgomery.)

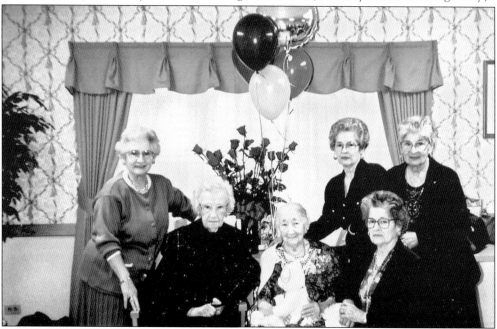

Lucy (Ebarb) Y'Barbo was born on November 26, 1893, and died April 5, 1994. As the last surviving member of the William and Stephanie Ebarb family, she is shown celebrating her 100th birthday. Pictured from left to right are Theo (Ebarb) Ezernack, Elvera (Martinez) Ebarb Procell, Lucy (Ebarb) Y'Barbo, Ruth (Ebarb) Loupe, Kathryn (Ebarb) Boudreaux, and Vivian Ebarb. (Courtesy of Karen Montgomery.)

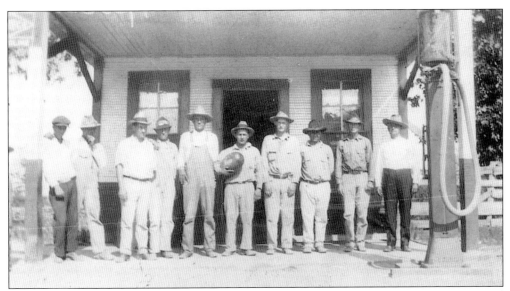

This picture was taken in front of the first Paul Ebarb store, built in Ebarb in 1925. Later Paul moved his store to Zwolle. From left to right are two unidentified, William Ebarb, Frank Procell, Dan Etheridge, Phillip Ebarb, George Sepulvado, John Nigreville, Paul Ebarb, and Ernest Procell. (Courtesy of Karen Montgomery.)

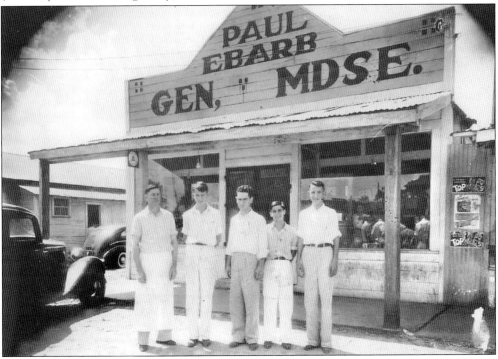

This Ebarb store was located on the main street in Zwolle. Cars were becoming more available, and streets were being paved. Posing for a picture from left to right are Simon L. Ebarb, Roy Martinez, J. O. Ebarb, Elmo Ebarb, and the future Fr. George Martinez (the first priest from Zwolle area). Simon Ebarb had begun his career as a butcher, which he held for more than 30 years. (Courtesy of Karen Montgomery.)

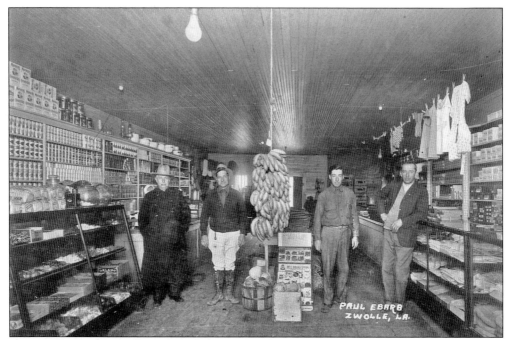

Posing inside the Paul Ebarb Store from left to right are William Ebarb, Pat Ebarb, Paul Ebarb, and George Martinez. This store was built around 1927 and later burned in the 1930s when robbers using matches for light accidentally set the store on fire. The entire store was destroyed. (Courtesy of Marie Polk.)

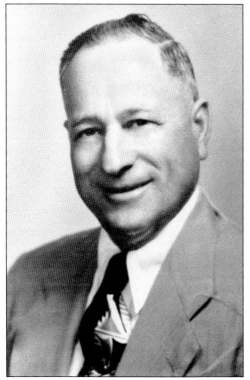

Paul Ebarb (1891–1966) was the son of William and Stephanie Ebarb. With $75, Ebarb opened his first store in Ebarb. He later moved the store to Zwolle; it consisted of a grocery market and dry goods section. Among Paul's accomplishments were being a school board member for 40 years, a member of the Zwolle Town Council, an astute businessman, and a member of several religious organizations at St. Joseph's Church. (Courtesy of Kathryn Boudreaux.)

Jessie Patrick Ebarb was born on March 17, 1920, and died February 6, 1943. He entered World War II to make the world safe for democracy. He was killed tragically when his plane crashed into the sea. (Courtesy of Kathryn Boudreaux.)

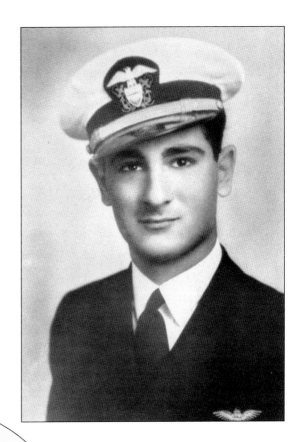

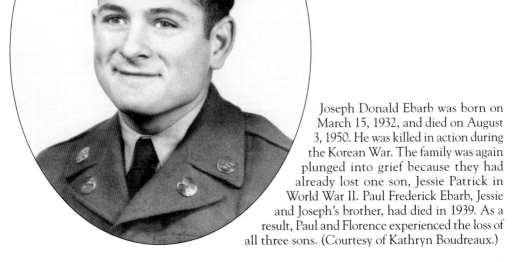

Joseph Donald Ebarb was born on March 15, 1932, and died on August 3, 1950. He was killed in action during the Korean War. The family was again plunged into grief because they had already lost one son, Jessie Patrick in World War II. Paul Frederick Ebarb, Jessie and Joseph's brother, had died in 1939. As a result, Paul and Florence experienced the loss of all three sons. (Courtesy of Kathryn Boudreaux.)

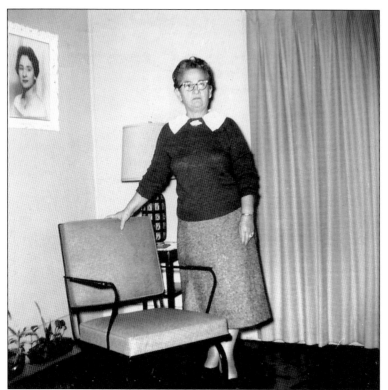

Florence (Ferguson) Ebarb was the daughter of John and Josephine (Sepulvado) Ferguson. She was mother of a large family: Jessie, Paul Frederick, Joseph Donald, Ruth, Kathryn, Vivian, Theo, Polly, and Frances. She worked many years in St. Theresa's Circle and was treasurer for the Altar Society. Twice she was a Gold Star Mother by reason of losing two sons in the defense of their country. (Courtesy of John C. and Carla Ebarb.)

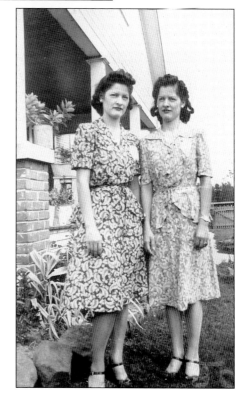

These twin sisters, Ruth (Ebarb) Loupe, left, and Kathryn (Ebarb) Boudreaux (born June 17, 1921), are the daughters of Paul Ebarb and Florence Ferguson. Ruth married Rogers Loupe, and Kathryn married Johnny Boudreaux. Both have lived in Zwolle for many years, with Johnny operating the Paul Ebarb Store and Rogers being a teacher and principal. They are pillars of the community, taking over duties when their parents became unable to do so. (Courtesy of Kathryn Boudreaux.)

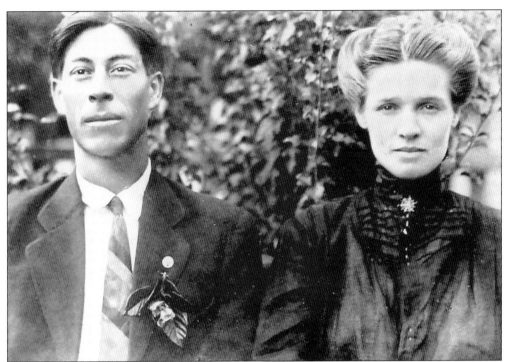

Cary Ebarb (September 23, 1885–September 23, 1924) and Louisa Ezernack (October 1, 1883–January 29, 1922) were married on February 11, 1907. Both died at an early age. Louisa died in childbirth when daughter Mary Louise was born. Two years later, Cary died of typhoid fever, leaving their nine children orphans. (Courtesy of Cody Bruce.)

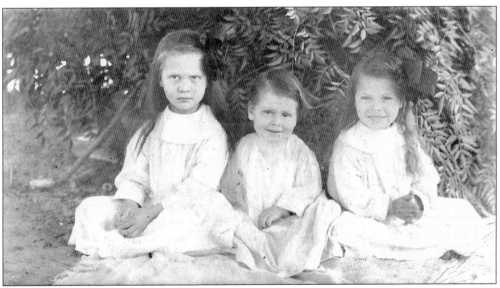

Posing for a picture are three daughters of Cary and Louisa (Ezernack) Ebarb. Pictured from left to right are Bertie, Alma, and Carrie. Bertie lived to be 96, Alma lived to be 63, and Carrie lived to be 95, unlike their parents who both died at age 39. Their three remaining siblings (as of 2006) are Julia (age 94), J. B. (age 92), and Bertha (age 86). (Courtesy of Marie Polk.)

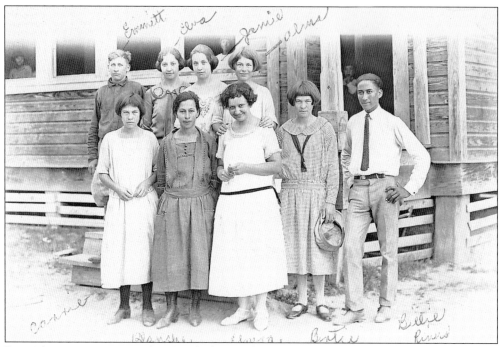

Posing for a group picture in their Sunday best in about 1920 are, from left to right, (first row) Carrie Ebarb, Blanche Ebarb, Elvera (Martinez) Ebarb, Bertie Ebarb, and Fred "Billy" Rivers; (second row) Emmett Ebarb, Elva Martinez, Janie Ebarb, and Alma Ebarb. (Courtesy of Marie Polk.)

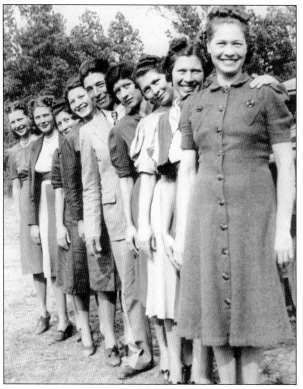

Pictured at a family gathering in the 1940s are the nine children of Cary and Louisa (Ezernack) Ebarb. From left to right are Mary Louise, Bertha, Florence, Elvia "Kate," John Bernard, Julia, Alma Bernice, Carrie, and Bertie Leona. They were lined up in order of age with Mary Louise being the baby in the family. Their mother died when Bertie was 15 years old, and their father died of typhoid fever two years later. (Courtesy of Cody Bruce.)

Shown in the picture are John C. and Carla Ebarb, who purchased the half-acre on which the Ebarb Fire Station is located. They donated it to the North Sabine Fire Station in March 2006. John and Carla were honored to be able to take part in community expansion because the fire station represents their special interest as firefighters and first responders. (Courtesy of John C. and Carla Ebarb.)

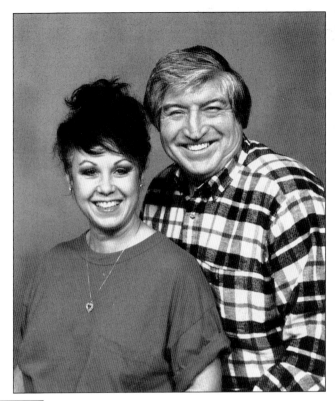

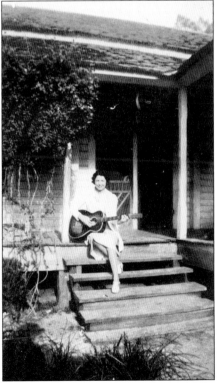

Lula Mae Longoria is shown playing the guitar at the home of Peter Ebarb. She was a schoolteacher at Ebarb who boarded at Peter Ebarb's home during the 1930s and 1940s. Very few people had cars in those days; therefore, the teachers had to board with someone who lived near the school. (Courtesy of Pauline Ebarb.)

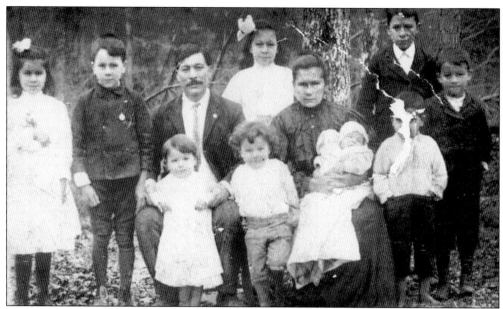

This family photograph, taken around 1911, shows the family of Phillip (1880–1928) and Mary (Sepulvado) Ebarb (1880–1961). From left to right are (first row) Edna, Albert, Phillip holding Ellis, Phillip Jr., Mary holding Jessie, Billy, and Clarence; (second row) Blanche and Walter. (Courtesy of Travis Ebarb Jr.)

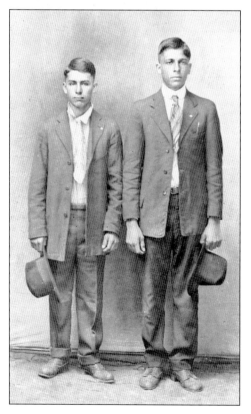

Pictured from left to right are Walter Ebarb (March 12, 1898–April 23, 1966), son of Phillip and Mary (Sepulvado) Ebarb, and George Procell, who later married Elvera (Martinez) Ebarb. Walter married Mattie M. Meshell. Their children are Verna and George Hobert Ebarb. (Courtesy of Ione Durr.)

Pictured are Edna (left, January 9, 1903–January 19, 1994) and Blanche (January 31, 1900–February 9, 1995). They were the daughters of Phillip and Mary (Sepulvado) Ebarb. This may have been their first communion picture, which occurred at about 12 years of age. More than one in a family would take part in baptisms, confirmations, first communions, or matrimony when a visiting priest made his rounds. (Courtesy of Iva Lee Meshell.)

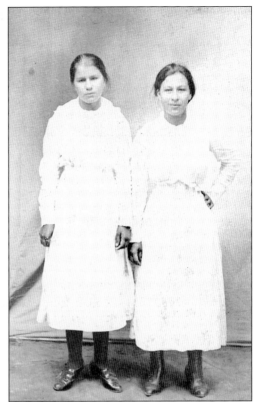

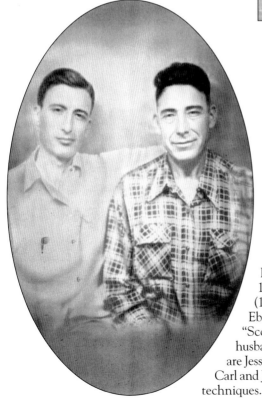

Pictured are cousins Carl "Tutt" Ebarb (left, 1917–1951) and Jessie "Hacker" Sepulvado (1904–1953). Carl was the husband of Minnie Ebarb (1920–2004). Their children are Richard T. "Scooter," Elsie, Vernon, and Wilma. Jessie was the husband of Mary Leone (1909–1978). Their children are Jessie B., Elizabeth Ann, Thurman, Ozell, and Edell. Carl and Jessie both died tragic deaths due to early logging techniques. (Courtesy of Thurman Sepulvado.)

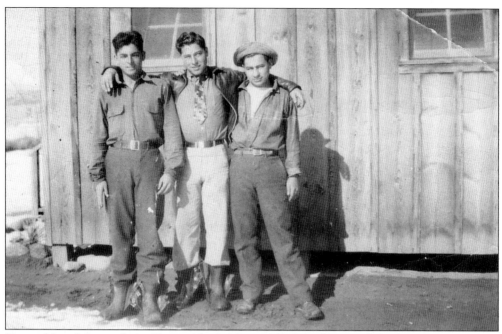

Pictured from left to right are Eugene Ebarb, Marvin Ebarb, and Leonard Ebarb at the CCC Camp in Utah in 1938. Being only 15 years of age, Leonard lied about his age in order to be hired. He was paid $30 a month. He received $5, and the remaining $25 was sent to his mother to help her support her family. (Courtesy of Pauline Ebarb.)

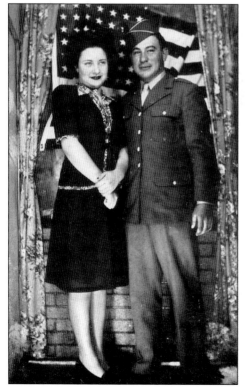

Leonard Ebarb (right) was the youngest child of Phillip and Mary (Sepulvado) Ebarb. As of 2006, he is the only surviving sibling of his family. He was drafted into the war during 1942 and served until he was discharged. Here he is pictured with an unidentified friend during World War II, where he took part in the Battle of the Bulge. He lived on the old Ebarb home place all his life until he was forced by ill health to enter the Toledo Nursing Center in Zwolle. (Courtesy of Leonard Ebarb.)

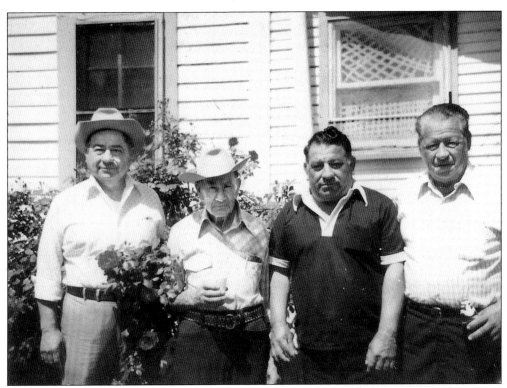

Shown in the picture from left to right are Leonard, Albert, Hilton, and John (Trib). They are four of Phillip and Mary (Sepulvado) Ebarb's sons. They lived near each other all their lives. They enjoyed meeting up at their brother Ellis Eugene's store, hunting, and fishing. (Courtesy of Leonard Ebarb.)

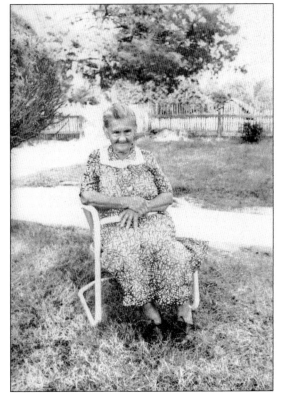

Mary Sepulvado married Phillip Ebarb in 1897. He died in 1928 at 48 years of age leaving her with many children and grandchildren to care for. Mary had to work very hard because there were no social services to help those in need at that time. She is remembered for donating one acre of land upon which the St. Ann's Church in Ebarb was built. (Courtesy of Leonard Ebarb.)

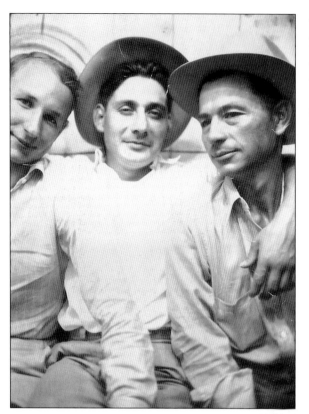

These three gentlemen are shown posing for a picture. Pictured from left to right are unidentified, Henry Lee (Tobe) Ebarb, and Ellis Eugene Ebarb. Henry is the son of Jacob and Irene (Rivers) Ebarb. Ellis is the son of Phillip and Mary (Sepulvado) Ebarb. (Courtesy of Michael LeRoy.)

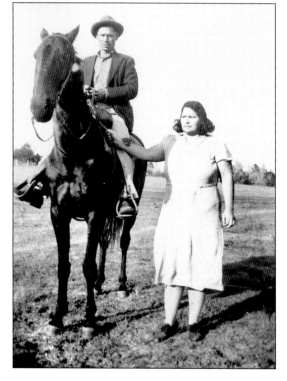

Ellis Eugene Ebarb was born September 9, 1909, and died November 24, 1994. He was married to Mary (Bessie) Rivers, who was born June 1, 1901, and died January 2, 1987. They had no biological children but raised their grandson, Michael LeRoy, who lives at the same homeplace today. Michael took care of his grandmother, who was bedridden for several years. (Courtesy of Michael LeRoy.)

Lucille (Procell) Ducote, born November 12, 1927, was the daughter of Tyne Procell and Mary (Bessie) Rivers. She was the mother of 16 children, including two sets of twins. Her children are Donnie, Michael, Gordon, Greg, Freddie, Alex, Deborah, Carl, Gary, Lucille, Donna, Edmund, Ralph, Tony, Alexandra, and an infant who died at birth. (Courtesy of Michael LeRoy.)

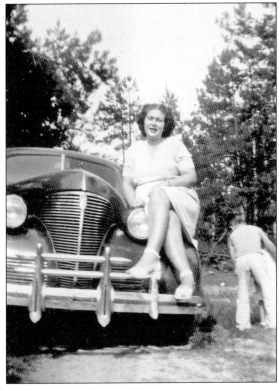

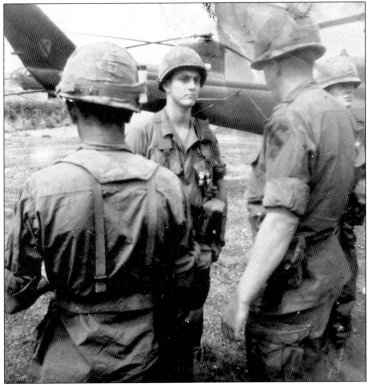

Michael LeRoy was born on November 14, 1945. From the time he was two weeks old, his grandparents, Ellis and Bessie Ebarb, raised him. Michael graduated from Ebarb High School in 1964. In the Vietnam War, he received several awards: Silver Star, Bronze Star, and Purple Heart. In this photograph, he is shown being awarded the Silver Star with comedienne Martha Rae present during the ceremony. (Courtesy of Michael LeRoy.)

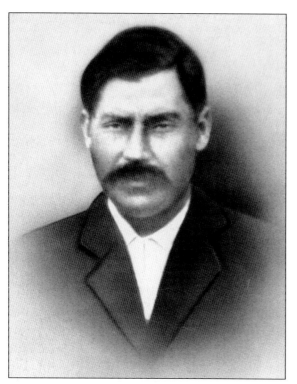

Francisco "Frank" Ebarb, son of Alcario and Martina Mattie (Ezernack) Ebarb, was born April 9, 1869. He married Mary Nigreville, and they had the following children: Martin, Frances, Mary, Margaret, Callie, Emmett, Della, Victoria, Elizabeth, Evelyn, and Annie Mae. With wife Mary Meshell, he had one daughter, Rita. (Courtesy of Rita McComic.)

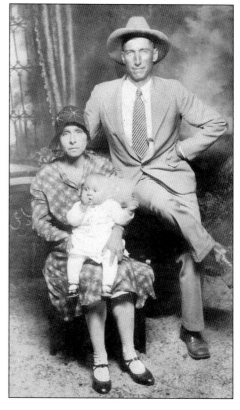

Pictured are Martin (1894–1982) and Inez (Laroux) (1899–1941) Ebarb with their daughter, Doris. In addition to Doris, they had the following children: June, Martin Jr., David, Herman, Eunice, Teresa, Joyce, Laverne, Frank, Delores, James, and Mildred. On June 5, 1943, Martin married Marie (Russell) Sepulvado, and they became parents to Pat, Peggy, Sheila, Marilyn, Brenda, Michael, Kenneth, Cindy, Roderick Anthony, Marsha, Shelly, Kimberly, and Greg. (Courtesy of Doris Leone.)

Josephine Ezernack was the daughter of Samuel Sharnac and Mary Lafitte. She married Teofilo Laroux and was the mother of four children. Their children were Malcom, Eva, Mary, and Sadie. Teofilo was a rancher and landowner. He was a notary public and served on the board of directors for the Bank of Zwolle. (Courtesy of Garthe Wright.)

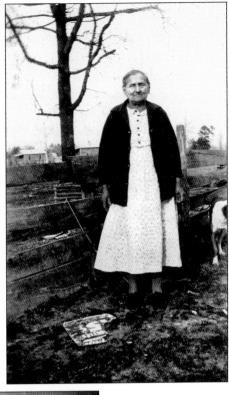

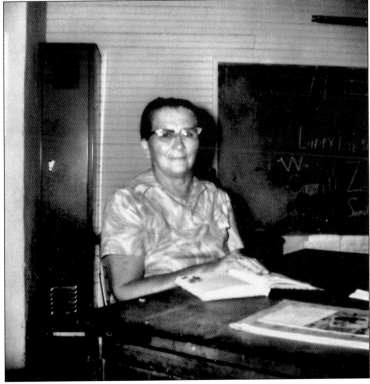

Eva (Laroux) Ebarb was a first-grade teacher. She taught reading and math to practically everyone beginning school at Ebarb High School. She taught first grade in the same school and classroom for 29 years. These were the days when the school had windows without screens, no air conditioners, and no computers. There was no such thing as kindergarten during this time either. (Courtesy of Raymond L. and Joan Ebarb.)

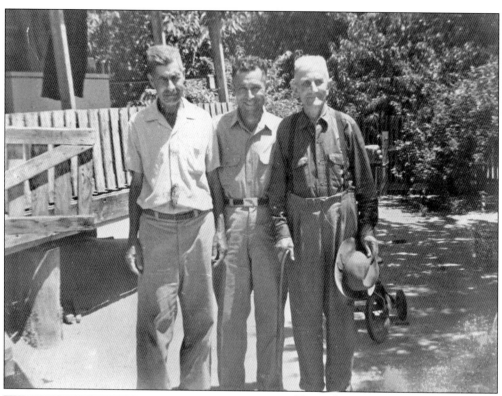

These three gentlemen pose for a picture in the yard of Henry B. Ebarb. Shown from left to right are Henry, Gene Nigreville, and John Nigreville. The Toledo Bend Reservoir flooded this area, and now the home place is gone forever under many feet of water. (Courtesy of Ann Rivers.)

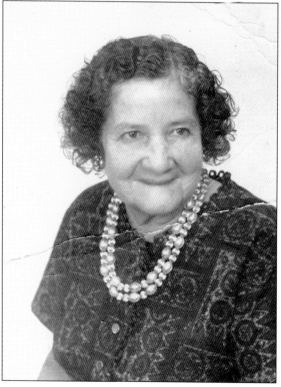

Francis (Sepulvado) Ebarb was born February 3, 1900, and died March 22, 1976. She was married to Henry B. Ebarb, and together they had the following children: Nellie, Aline, Shirley, J. W., Jessie, Johnny, Minnie, and Tony. Both Frances and her husband are buried in St. Joseph's Cemetery. (Courtesy of Ann Rivers.)

Pictured is Athanasius Boniface Ebarb in World War II. Known as Tony, he was the son of Henry B. and Francis (Sepulvado) Ebarb. He was born May 2, 1923, and died August 9, 2006. He married Winnie Rivers, who preceded him in death on December 20, 1986. Together they were parents of four children: Jerry, Judy, Tony, and Robert. (Courtesy of Joe Ebarb.)

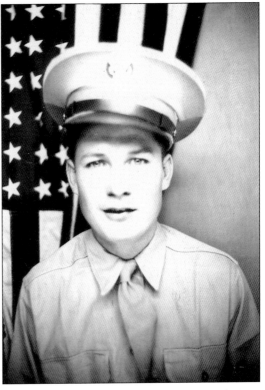

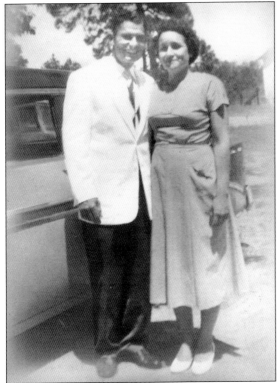

Johnny Ebarb and Catherine Paddie are shown posing for a picture. Johnny was the son of Henry B. Ebarb and Frances Sepulvado. Catherine's parents are John L. and Josephine Paddie. Johnny and Catherine were married on January 19, 1946. Their children are Ann, Larry, James, Charles Ray, and Rebecca. (Courtesy of Ann Rivers.)

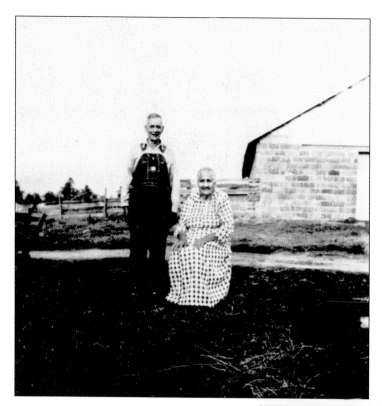

Henry Hilton Procell was born February 6, 1872, and died April 28, 1963. Henry's wife, Marcelina (Sepulvado) Procell, was born September 28, 1870, and died September 4, 1960. They were parents to Fred, Edna, Lucy, and Clarence. Marcelina had been married before to John Ezernack and had two children, Christina and Marie. (Courtesy of Ione Durr.)

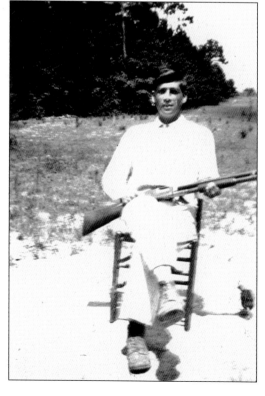

Homer Ezernack (August 28, 1899–April 17, 1958) is shown sitting proudly with his Winchester model 1897 shotgun. Homer is remembered as a carpenter who helped build the 1926 Ebarb High School. Most men and some women in Northwest Louisiana enjoy the sport of hunting rabbits, squirrel, raccoons, ducks, and deer. (Courtesy of Ione Durr.)

Edna (Procell) Ezernack, wife of Homer Ezernack, is shown proudly standing in a boat that she and her father made from a cypress log. She is in the Sabine River, which forms the boundary between Texas and Louisiana. People had to be creative and solve their own problems in order to survive. Overalls were work clothes then but today can be a fashion statement. (Courtesy of Ione Durr.)

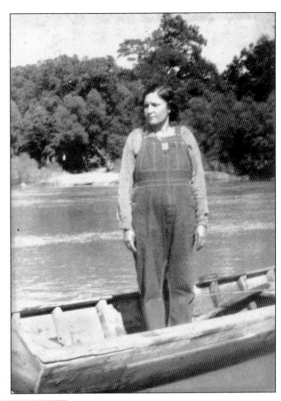

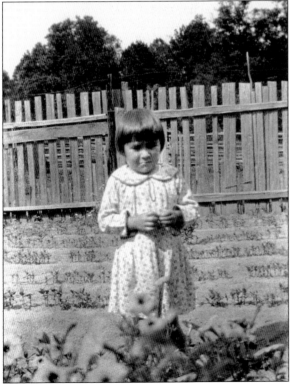

Dorothy Marie Ezernack is shown standing in the garden. She was the daughter of Homer and Edna (Procell) Ezernack. She was born August 15, 1930, and died October 20, 1981. She married Elmer Procell (1921–1996), the son of Sam and Pollie (Leone) Procell. They had six children, which included Jeffery, Ione, Velda, Gary, Amelia, and Leslie. (Courtesy of Ione Durr.)

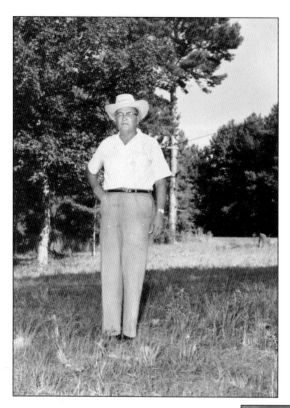

Albert Keelan Ezernack (December 16, 1901–October 2, 1984) was the son of Guadelupe Ezernack and Elva Ebarb. He married Ester Ezernack (September 2, 1909–February 2, 2003). She is the daughter of Joseph Ezernack and Hattie Ebarb. (Courtesy of John C. and Carla Ebarb.)

Norbert Ezernack was born in 1929. He was the son of Keelan and Ester Ezernack. He was a U.S. Army medic stationed in Germany. He died in a swimming accident there on July 4, 1952. He is buried in St. Joseph's Cemetery in Zwolle. (Courtesy of Vincent Ebarb.)

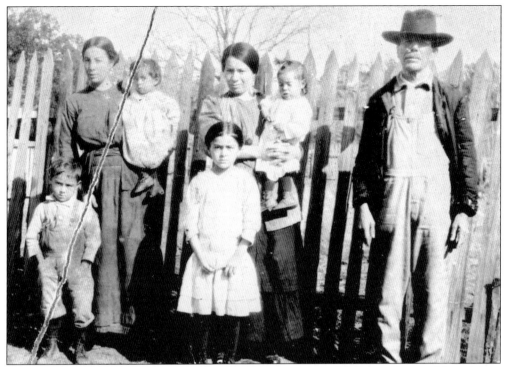

Posing against a picket fence was the family of Crescentio "C. C." Garcie. Pictured from left to right are (first row) Lawrence Malmay and Dollie Malmay; (second row) Margaret (Garcie) Malmay holding Earl Malmay, Elizabeth Garcie holding Pearl Malmay, and C. C. Garcie. (Courtesy of Pauline Ebarb.)

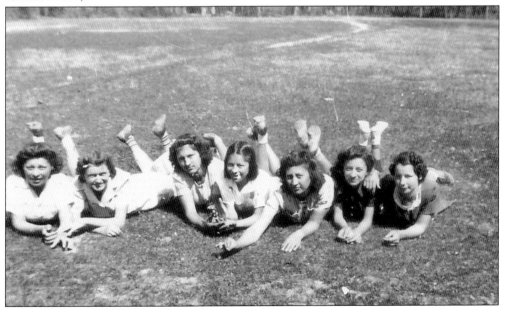

Maybe they are looking for four-leaf clovers or maybe they are just enjoying a warm spring day. Members of the group shown from left to right are Pauline Ebarb, Cecil Ebarb, Myrtie Sepulvado, Catherine Ebarb, Ruby Sepulvado, Patsy Ebarb, and Elvira Ebarb. (Courtesy of Pauline Ebarb.)

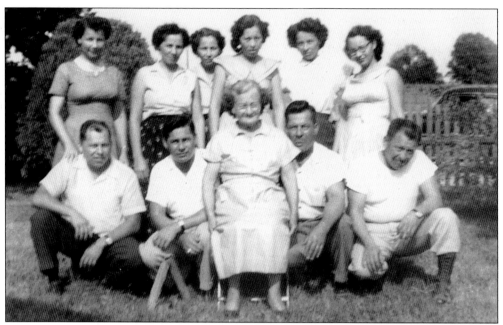

Elizabeth "Betsy" Ebarb (1888–1969) was married August 31, 1916, to Louis Ebarb (1877–1943). Betsy is shown sitting in the center. Pictured from left to right around here are (first row) Bernice, Joseph Raymond, Robert, and Earl; (second row) Elvira, Julia, Evelyn, Catherine, Pauline, and Mary Laverne. (Courtesy of Pauline Ebarb.)

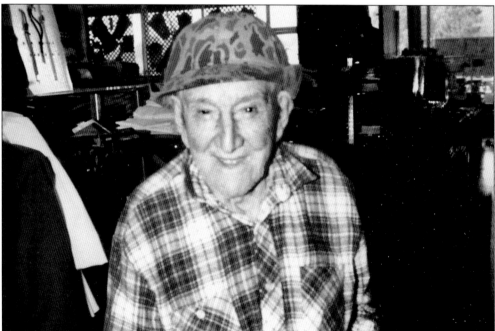

Henry Garcie (August 12, 1884–August 12, 1987), son of Jim Garcie and Dora Leone, was a World War I veteran. His children are Jack, Joseph, Curtis, James, Henry, David, Freddy, Annie Ruth, Barbara, and Ethel. His siblings were Jimmy, Juanita, Manuel, Ascencion, Salley, Frank, Eli, Mary, and George. Henry enjoyed playing the fiddle until his death. (Courtesy of Catherine Sepulvado.)

Standing on the railroad track, Ed Garcie poses in the snow (a rare occurrence in the Deep South). Ed (1910–1982), son of Frank Garcie and Nennie Meshell, married Louise Sepulvado. Their children are Mary Jane, Betty Jo, and Ella Faye. (Courtesy of Clifton Garcie.)

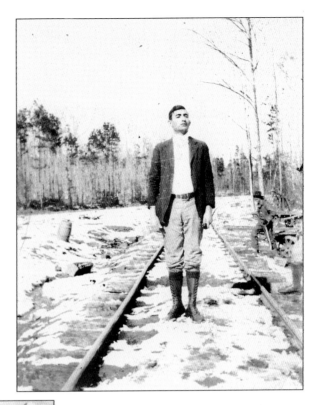

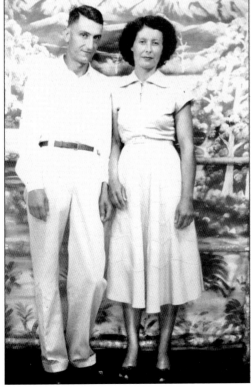

Bertie Sepulvado and Clifton Garcie pose for a picture in their younger days. Bertie was born September 11, 1918, and died June 11, 2002. Clifton, Bertie's husband, was born April 13, 1918. Clifton proved his devotion by taking care of Bertie during her long illness. Their children are Shirley, Pat, Chris, Doris Jean, and Joseph Clifton Jr. (Courtesy of Clifton Garcie.)

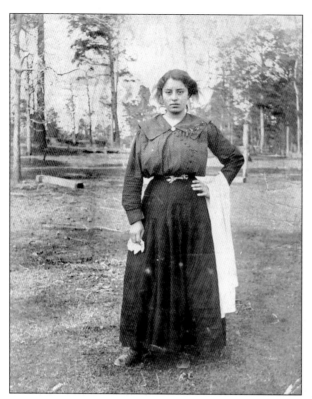

Martha "Thomasa" Malmay, daughter of Hosea Simon Bermea, was born December 8, 1890, and died August 23, 1973. She married Marceline Ebarb and was the mother of Henry M. Ebarb. This picture was taken on the banks of the Sabine River. (Courtesy of Clifton Garcie.)

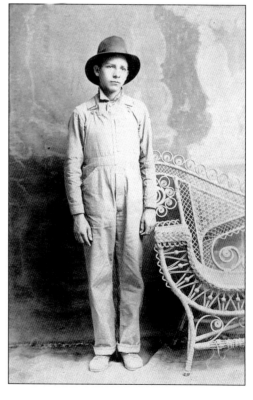

Steve Ebarb (1902–1994) was the son of H. M. Ebarb and Juana Sepulvado. He married Sarah Sepulvado (1896–1980), daughter of Willie Sepulvado and Stefana Bebee, on June 15, 1928. Their children are Fannie, Clifton, Joanna, Herman, Merlene, Maggie, Rosie, and Mary Ann. (Courtesy of Carolyn Williams.)

Rupert Ebarb (1913–1991) and Annie Procell (1914–1971) pose for a picture. Together they raised seven children: Carolyn, Patsy, Janie, Gloria, Howard, Sybil, and Linnie. Rupert was a natural-born hunter and trapper. He was also a logger, farmer, and rancher. Annie loved to sew, embroider, quilt, and read. (Courtesy of John C. and Carla Ebarb.)

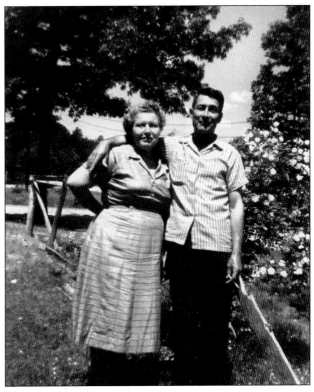

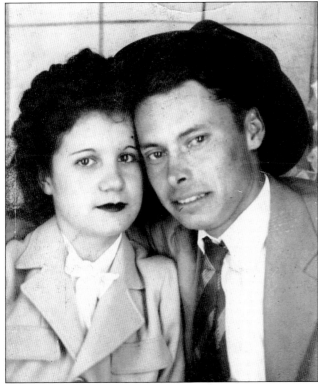

Shown in the picture are T. J. Ebarb and Rosalie Procell, who were married on October 26, 1946. T. J.'s parents were Manuel Ebarb and Florence Procell. Rosalie's parents were Ernest Procell and Mary Sepulvado. T. J., short for Teofilo John, was named in honor of Teofilo Laroux. Their children are Troy, Ronald, Donald, Clayton, Michael, Peggy, and Bobby. (Courtesy of T. J. and Rosalie Ebarb.)

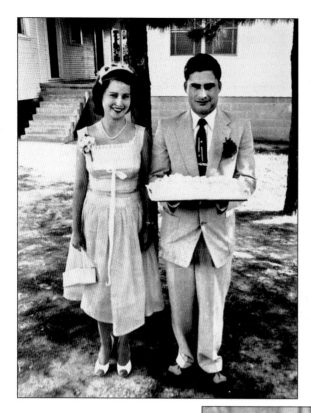

Murray "Bill" Ebarb, brother of Teofilo John, is shown holding the wedding cake after his marriage to Emma Jean Procell, daughter of Joe William Procell and Sylvia Rivers, on July 13, 1955. Bill was born May 18, 1931, and died October 26, 1997. Emma Jean was born December 16, 1938. Bill and Emma had the following children: Freda, Daigle, Cheryl, Anita, and Karla. (Courtesy of Emma Jean Ebarb.)

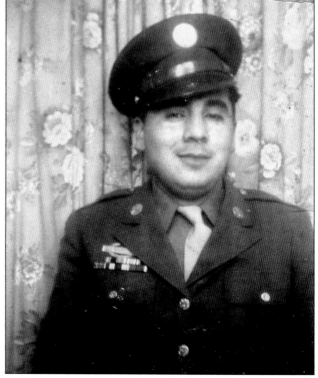

Reese Ebarb, a private first-class in the army during World War II, is shown in his uniform. He was the son of Fred Ebarb and Mary Emma (Meshell) Ebarb and grandson of Marceline Ebarb. His brothers and sisters were Mary Hazel, Thomas Whitney Sr., Mertie Mae, Mattie, and Arvel William "Duce." (Courtesy of Linda Champion.)

John Brown Jr. was born August 12, 1877, and died in California around 1948. His wife was Lou Ella Garcie, who was born in 1895 and died December 15, 1918. John Brown Curve, a dangerous place on Highway 482 where many deadly accidents have occurred, was named after John Brown because his house was located near it. (Courtesy of James Brown.)

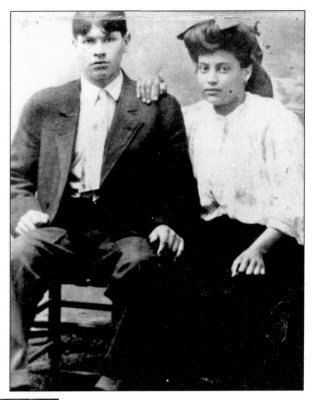

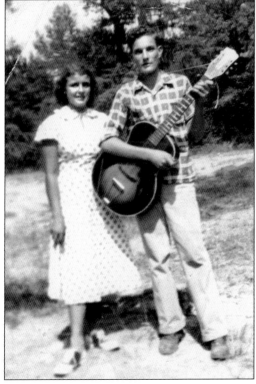

Thomas Brown, known as "Ditty," poses with his trusty guitar in the company of Catherine Ebarb, daughter of Ira Ebarb Sr. and Evelyn Rebecca Sepulvado. Thomas is the son of Thad Brown and Mary Campbell. (Courtesy of Dorothy King.)

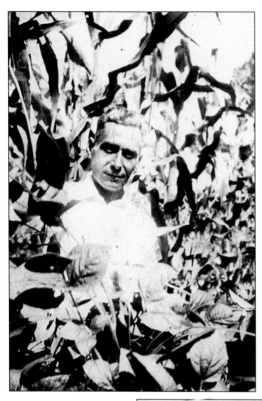

Beto Castillo was born August 5, 1896. He is shown posing in a cornfield at the family's old home place. This photograph was taken in 1945. He died on February 2, 1978, and is buried at St. Ann's Cemetery in Ebarb. Incarnacion, his father, was a full-blooded Native American who came to Ebarb. Incarnacion married a local girl and remained there for the rest of his life. (Courtesy of Theresa [Castillo] Henderson).

Lucy Procell was born on Palm Sunday, April 5, 1906. This photograph of Lucy was taken in 1956. She was the daughter of Marcelina Sepulvado and Henry Procell. She was married to Beto Castillo, son of Incarnacion Castie and Mary Ellen Procell, on November 4, 1922. They had the following children: Joseph, Anthony, Jessie, Charles, Mary Lurline, Carman, Mary Theresa, Louis, Alvis, Gloria, Virginia, and Glenn. (Courtesy of Theresa [Castillo] Henderson).

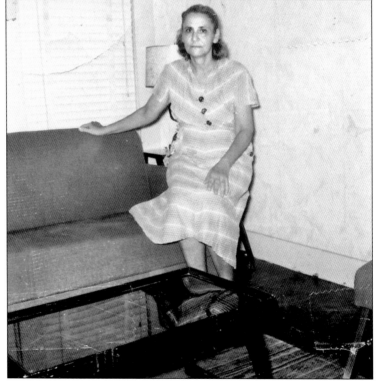

Edward Slavko Crnkovic and his wife, Frazine, pose for a picture possibly in the early 1920s. Ed, an immigrant from Yugoslavia, was born January 19, 1884, and died November 20, 1963. Frazine, daughter of Peter Ebarb and Josephine Longoria, was born November 25, 1902, and died February 1, 1985. Their children were Steve, Joseph, Johnny, Frank, Pete, Wilburn, Donald, Helen, Josephine, and Lois. (Courtesy of Pauline Ebarb.)

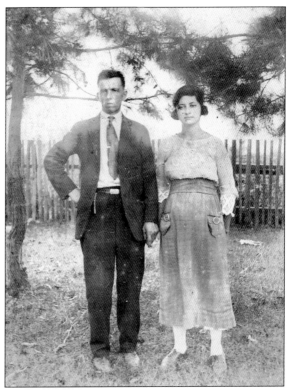

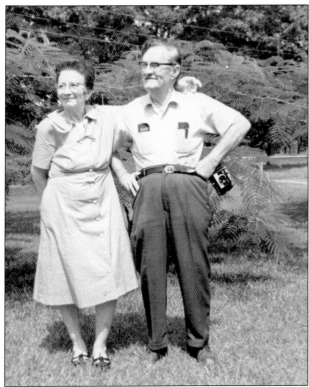

Maggie Ebarb poses with her husband, Anthony E. Kezerle. Anthony is of Croatian descent. His parents came from Yugoslavia. He was born in 1889 and died in 1974. Maggie, whose parents were Peter Ebarb and Josephine Longoria, was born in 1900 and died in 1974. Their children were Theresa, Lloyd, Loran, Agnes, Don, Anthony, Katherine, and Sebastian. (Courtesy of Theresa Sepulvado.)

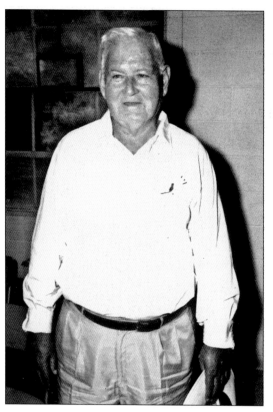

Frank Leone (1893–1974) was the son of Eli Leone and Mary Ann Young. He married Lena Sepulvado, and they became the parents of Louisa, Mary Ann, Wilson, Doug, Frank, and Blanche. His siblings were Pat, Obra, Mattie, Oma, Lorenza, Polly, and Ester. His half-brothers and -sisters were Helen, Andrew, Betty, Floriana, Bonnie, Lorena, and Gustava. (Courtesy of Muriel Rivers.)

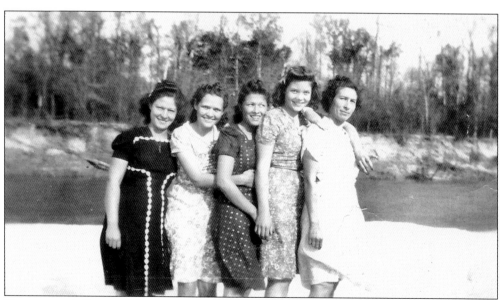

These young ladies posed for a picture by the Sabine River. Pictured from left to right are Blanche Leone, Evelyn (Williams) Bragg, Mary Ann (Leone) Rivers, Wanda Williams, and Louise (Leone) Ebarb. Blanche, Mary Ann, and Louise were the daughters of Frank Leone and Lena Sepulvado. Evelyn and Wanda were also sisters. (Courtesy of Muriel Rivers.)

Antonia Margaret Ebarb (December 25, 1856–May 22, 1960) was the daughter of Hosea Severo Y'Barbo and Mary Lou "Viviana" Procell. She married Leonard (called "Leon" or "Nie") Manshack. Their eight children were Sevedo, Ellen, Joseph, Tom, George, Mary Lodie, Dora, and Manuel. Margaret lived to be 104 years of age. She is buried in St. Ann's Cemetery in Ebarb. (Courtesy of Sue Vines.)

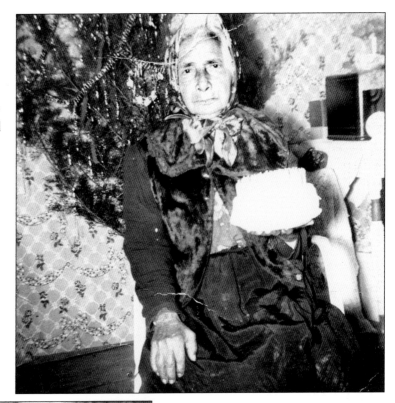

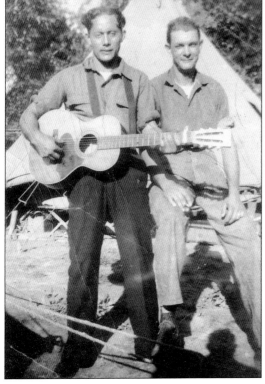

This picture was taken in 1933 at a Civilian Conservation Corps Camp. Pictured from left to right are Manuel Manshack with his guitar and an unidentified friend. The CCC Camps, one of the popular programs in the 1930s, were established by Franklin D. Roosevelt's New Deal to help unemployed people. Earning $30 per month, the men were required to send $25 of their salary to their families. (Courtesy of Travis Ebarb Jr.)

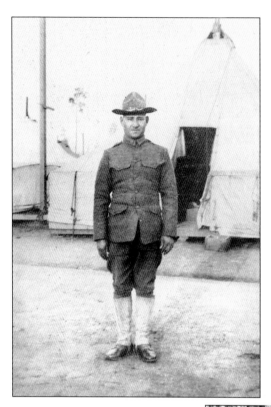

Tom Manshack is shown posing for a picture in his uniform at a camp during World War I. He was born April 2, 1892, and died November 12, 1985. He is buried in St. Catherine's Cemetery in Noble, Louisiana. Tom proudly served his country in the war that was supposed to end all wars. (Courtesy of Joe [Dee] Procell.)

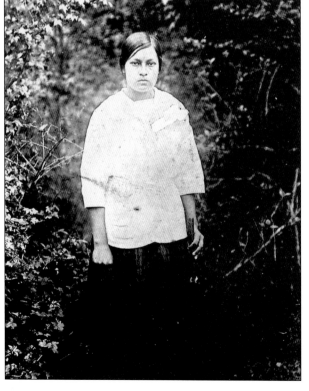

Ella Paddie (1896–1936) is shown posing for a picture. She is the daughter of Pete Paddie and Mattie Ebarb. She married Tom Manshack. During the time she was pregnant, a fire broke out near their home. She tried to put it out and as a result lost her baby, and she died of complications from this tragic event. (Courtesy of Lois Manshack.)

Manuel Joseph Manshack (1912–1994) is shown posing with his wife, Maybell Elizabeth Paddie (1918–2003), whom he married on November 13, 1937. Children born to them were Manuel John "M. J.", Sam Harvey, Patricia Ann, Molly Ruth, and Margaret Sue. Manuel, a timber contractor, worked in the woods his entire life. Maybell was a homemaker and took care of her family. (Courtesy of Travis Ebarb Jr.)

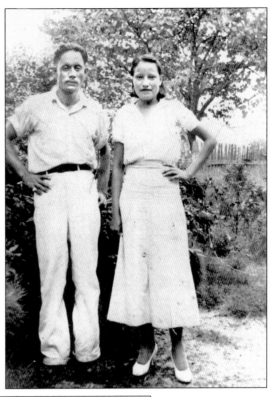

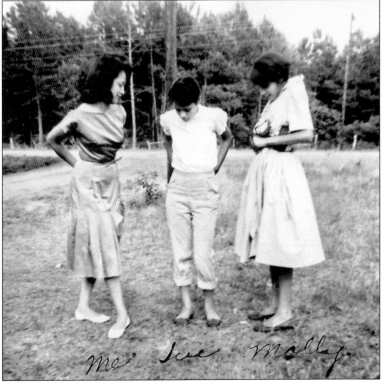

Getting ready for a picture and dressed in the latest fashions for 1959 are the three daughters of Manuel Joseph Manshack and Maybell Elizabeth Paddie. Pictured from left to right are Patricia Ann, Margaret Sue, and Molly Ruth. (Courtesy of Patsy Ebarb.)

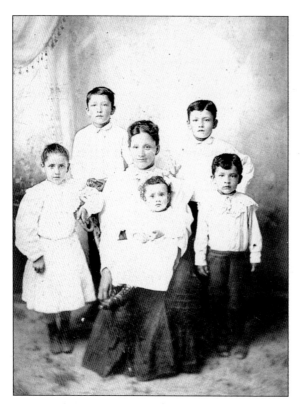

Shown posing for a family picture are Mary Ferguson Martinez (1875–1938) and her children. Pictured from left to right are (first row) Elva, Mary Martinez holding Elvera, and Rupert; (second row) George and Walter. Brother Herman Martinez had not been born yet. Mary's husband was Steve Martinez Jr. (1875–1944), son of Estevan Martinez (1847–1917) and Juana Sepulvado (1851–1898). (Courtesy of Marie Polk.)

All decked out in their Easter finery were the children of Steve Jr. and Mary Martinez. Pictured from left to right are Elva, Rupert, and Elvera. Elva's son became a priest; Rupert was 12 years old when he died in 1914; Elvera became a teacher at Ebarb School and died in 2000 at the age of 96. (Courtesy of Marie Polk.)

Taking time for a photograph are, from left to right, (first row) Emmett E. Meshell and Steve Martinez Jr.; (second row) George Martinez, Walter Martinez, and Jimmy Garcie. Steven was the father of George and Walter Martinez. This photograph was taken in Beaumont, Texas, while the men were on a trip to Port Arthur, Texas, to see a whale that had washed up on the beach in 1916. (Courtesy of Iva Lee Meshell.)

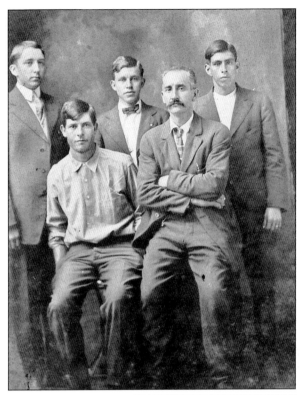

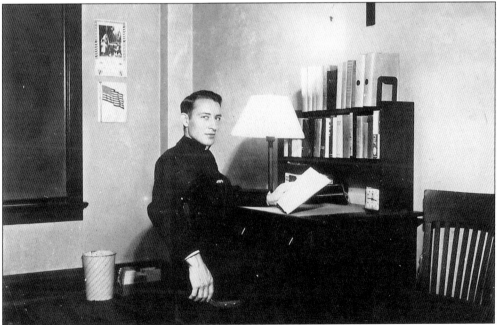

Msgr. George Martinez was the first native son of Zwolle to be ordained. He was born January 20, 1920, and died June 23, 1997. He was the son of George Martinez and Fannie Ebarb. His siblings are Theresa, Joe Pat, Steve, Anthony, and Roy. He is buried in St. Joseph's Cemetery in Zwolle, Louisiana. (Courtesy of Marie Polk.)

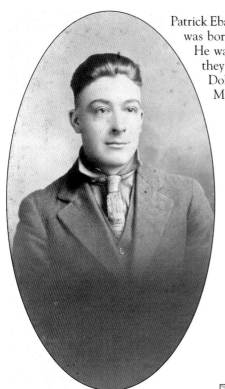

Patrick Ebarb, son of William and Stephanie (Nigreville) Ebarb, was born February 13, 1900, and died on March 15, 1936. He was married about 1918 to Elvera Martinez. Together they had five children: Elvera Marie, Edith Patricia, Eloise Dolores, Hazel Gloria, and Patrick Allen. (Courtesy of Marie Polk.)

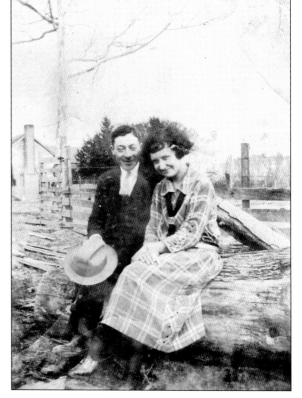

Pat Ebarb and Elvera Martinez are shown during their courting days. Courting took place at the girl's house in front of the entire family or at the country dances, usually on the weekend. Dances too were very well chaperoned. A fireplace or chimney pictured on the house in the background was the primary means of heating homes. (Courtesy of Marie Polk.)

Homer Martinez, son of Gilbert Martinez and Gertrude Sepulvado, served in World War II, was a Knight of Columbus member, and was a school board member for 24 years. Homer is credited with keeping Ebarb School open when the school's closure was being considered. Bertie Mae, daughter of Raymond Campbell and Erlene Sepulvado, was a lector, rosary leader, Eucharistic minister, and a member of the Liturgy Committee and St. Theresa's Circle. (Courtesy of Bertie Mae Martinez.)

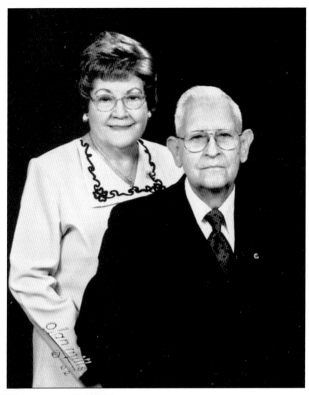

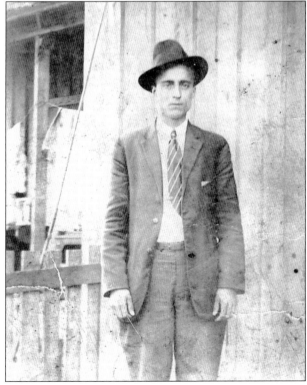

George Sylvester Leone was the son of Luciano and Hilaria (Sepulvado) Leone. His siblings were Charlie, Josephine, Marcelina, Peter, Jessie, John, Ellen, Henry, Stella, Edna, and Thomas. George married Claudia Varnell, and they were parents to Clara, Ruby, Ruth, and Delphi. Claudia died in 1922 and George in 1936. (Courtesy of Cody Bruce.)

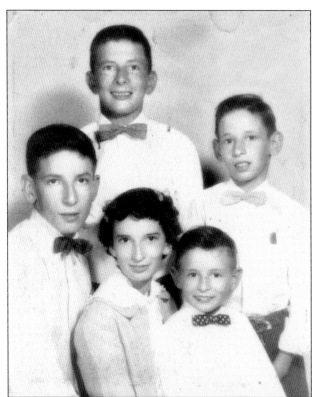

The children of Granvil "Chooch" and Catherine (Sepulvado) Martinez pose for a picture. From left to right are (first row) Granvil Joseph "Pie," Ann, and Pat; (second row) Albert Thomas "B. B." and Eddie. Ann lives in Florida, while all the boys live in Louisiana. (Courtesy of G. J. "Pie" Martinez.)

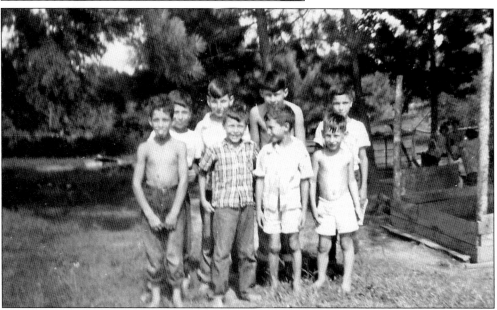

Having fun in the "good ole' summertime" were these cousins. Pictured from left to right are (first row) Johnny Rivers, Sammy Rivers, Phillip Joe Rivers, and Eddie Martinez; (second row) Thomas Rivers, Granvil Joseph "Pie" Martinez, Roy Rivers, and Freddy Rivers. Bare feet, swimming holes, long summer days, and lots of cousins to play and wrestle with—what more could a young boy in the 1950s need to be happy? (Courtesy of Mary Lucille Rivers.)

One of the original dough boys in World War I (the War to End All Wars) was George Meshell, brother of businessman Emmett E. Meshell. This photograph is of historical significance because very few photographs from World War I could be found. George died under mysterious circumstances several years after the war was over. (Courtesy of Iva Lee Meshell.)

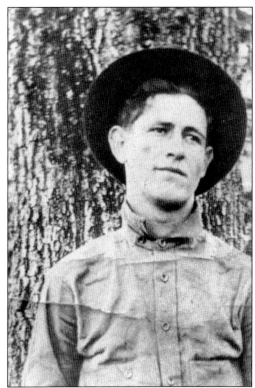

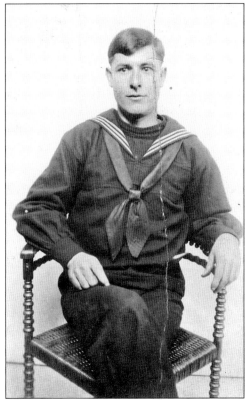

Emmett E. Meshell (1894–1983) posed in his navy uniform in 1918. He married Iva Lee Meshell in 1950 and had four sons: David, Dennis, DeWayne, and Donnie. Emmett bought 40 acres of land when he was 18 years old. When the First Bank of Zwolle closed during the Depression, he lost his land. When the bank reopened, he bought his land back. (Courtesy of Iva Lee Meshell.)

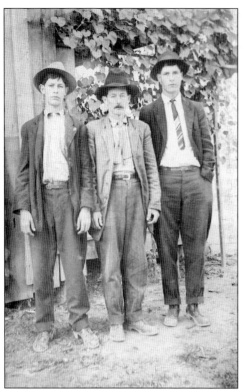

Posing in front of English ivy and decked out in their Sunday clothes are, from left to right, George Meshell, John Leone, and Emmett E. Meshell. Felt hats for men, narrow ties, and baggy pants seemed to be the latest fashion. George and Emmett were brothers. They were both in the service in World War I. (Courtesy of Iva Lee Meshell.)

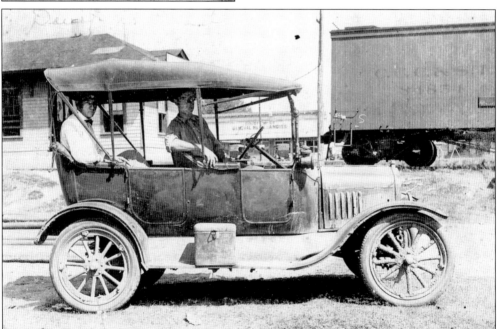

Emmett E. Meshell is the driver in one of the early automobiles in Sabine Parish. He is accompanied by ? Dover, a local Zwolle merchant. In the background is the train depot, which is over 100 years old. This picture must have been taken before 1927 since Paul Ebarb's store is not there. (Courtesy of Iva Lee Meshell.)

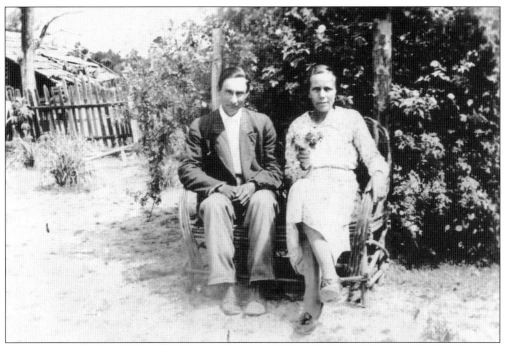

John Sidney Paddie (1888–1979) poses with his wife, Molly Elizabeth Brown (1893–1944), in the yard of their home. Their home was located above Converse, west of the Cross Roads, at the end of the gravel road. John and Molly were the parents of Sam, Monroe, Mary, Maybell, Rita, Audrey, and George. (Courtesy of Travis Ebarb Jr.)

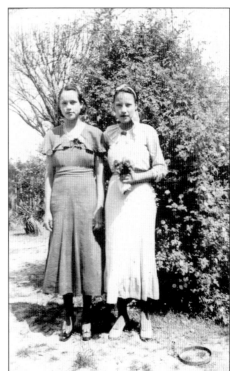

Shown are Rita (left) and Maybell Paddie, twin sisters, who were born on February 23, 1918. They were the daughters of John Sidney and Molly (Brown) Paddie. Together with their sister, Mary, the twins were known as the "Sidney Girls." This name was used to distinguish them from the daughters of the other John Paddie. John was a common Paddie name at the time, even among those not related. (Courtesy of Sue Vines.)

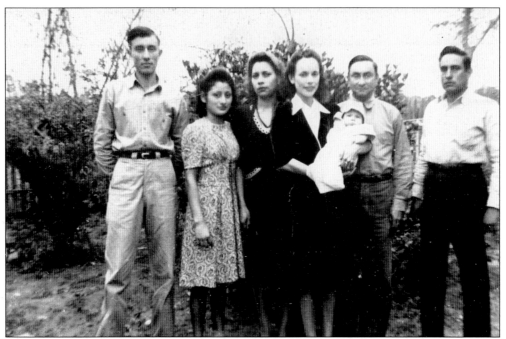

Paddie relatives pose for a picture. Shown from left to right are George "G. C."; Josie Marie (daughter of Richard Paddie, John Paddie's brother); Audrey; Rita, holding son Gary; John Sidney Paddie; and Monroe. A musically inclined family, the Paddies loved to go to the old country dances, a major source of entertainment in those days. (Courtesy of Sue Vines.)

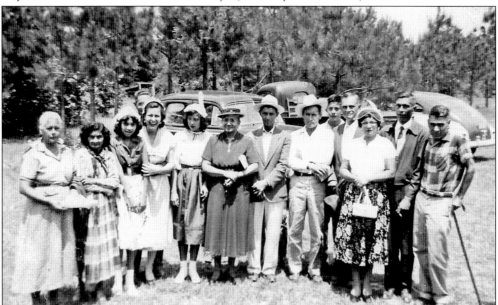

This group of people in their Sunday clothes probably had been to church either at Round Lake's Our Lady of Mount Carmel Church or St. Catherine's near Sulphur Springs. Pictured from left to right, they are Rosie Meshell, Elva Procell, Lucy Brown, Amos Manshack (partially hidden), Elsie Manshack, unidentified, Addie Ebarb, Lou Ebarb, Joe Meshell, Joe Procell Jr., Joe Procell Sr., Carrie Paddie, Charlie Paddie, and Tom Procell. (Courtesy of Ernest "Chay" Procell.)

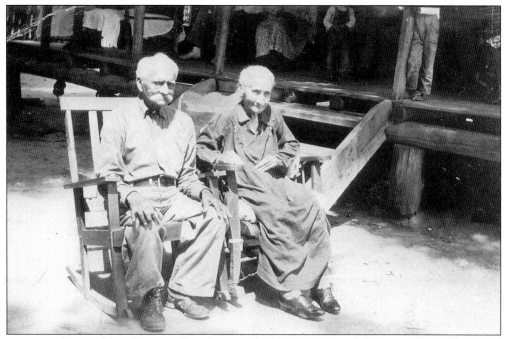

Posing in their rocking chairs in their front yard are Bush (left) and Christina (Procell) Paddie. Their house was a rustic cabin that their family had built for them. Bush was born May 11, 1861, and died September 30, 1944. Christina was born July 25, 1870, and died December 11, 1943. Their children include Lizzie, John L., and Steve. (Courtesy of Ann Rivers.)

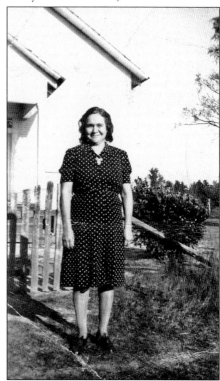

Josephine (Santos) Paddie was the daughter of Crescentia Procell and Pete Santos. She was born December 24, 1900, and died March 4, 1988. She is buried in St. Catherine's Cemetery in Noble, Louisiana. She was the wife of John Ludry Paddie. Their children are Catherine, Josephine, Christine, Huey, Dewey, John T., Pete, Yvonne Elvia, Jewel, Laverne, and Esther. (Courtesy of Catherine Ebarb.)

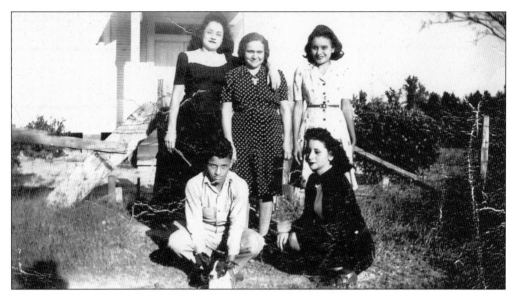

The Paddie family lived near St. Catherine's Church near Sulphur Springs, Louisiana. The family is shown posing for a picture. Pictured from left to right are (seated) Dewey and Jewel; (standing) Catherine, Josephine, and Christine. This picture was taken in 1946. (Courtesy of Catherine Ebarb.)

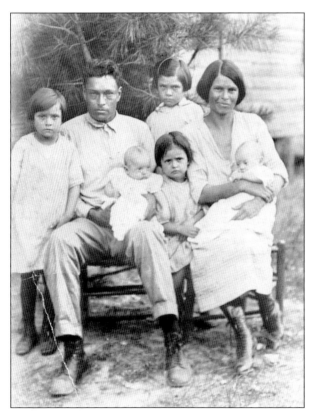

Posing for a family photograph are Joe Foster and Rosa Lena (Procell) Paddie. Pictured from left to right are Cora, Joe holding Lovell, Rosa Mae, Bernice (between the babies), and Rosa Lena holding Odell. This photograph was taken in 1927 before Willard and Shane were born. Joe Foster was born February 15, 1892, and died February 22, 1980. His wife, Rosa Lena, was born March 18, 1898, and died April 22, 1991. (Courtesy of Rose Mary Procell.)

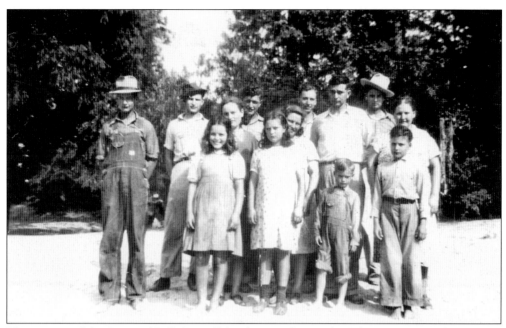

This picture of the Sam and Polly Procell family was taken at the Sabine River on July 28, 1942. Pictured from left to right are (first row) Maudie, Lenora, Winnie, Mary Ann, Roy, and Bruce; (second row) Solan, Herman, Elmer, Jake, Sam, Joe William, and Polly. The family had to move when Toledo Bend Reservoir was created. (Courtesy of Solan Procell.)

Sam Procell and his wife, Polly, pose for a picture with granddaughter Linda Acklin. This picture was taken at their old home place before Toledo Bend Lake was created. This picture must have been taken on a Sunday because the group was dressed in their Sunday clothes. The photographer was Solan Procell. (Courtesy of Solan Procell.)

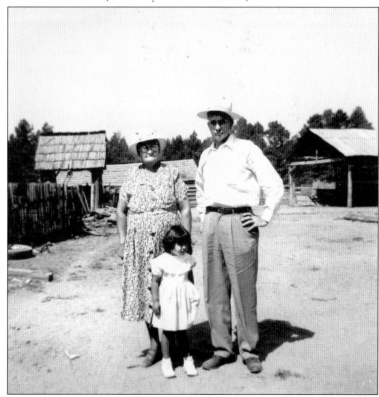

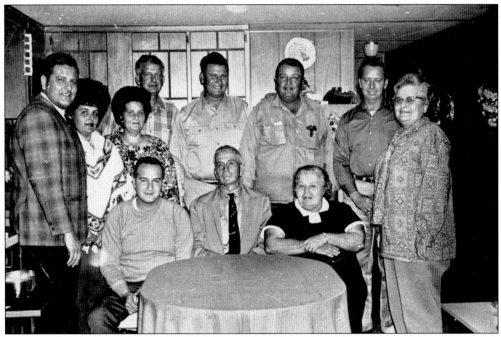

Posing for a family picture are the children of Sam Procell and Polly Leone. Shown from left to right are (seated) Roy, Sam, and Annie (Procell) Ebarb; (standing) Bruce, Maudie (Procell) Sepulvado Woodruff, Winnie (Procell) Acklin, Solan, Herman, Elmer, Jake, and Lena. Polly died on December 22, 1953. (Courtesy of Solan Procell.)

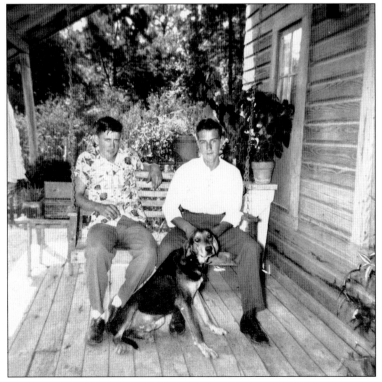

Posing on a swing on the front porch of Louis and Elizabeth "Betsy" Ebarb's home are Joseph "C. B." Lee Ebarb (left) and Roy Procell. Their faithful canine friend sits near them. Joseph Lee is the son of Joseph Sr. and Florence Procell. Roy is the son of Sam and Pollie Procell. (Courtesy of Solan Procell.)

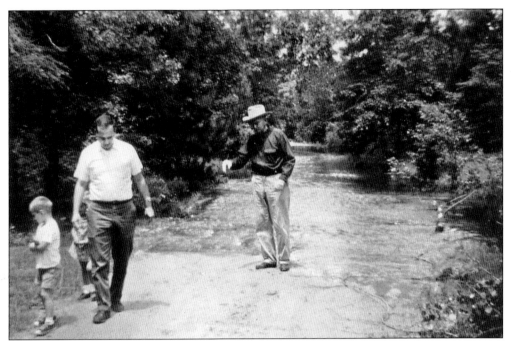

Sam Procell (center) is shown measuring how far the water from Toledo Bend Lake has risen. This area was below Fred Procell's home site. Steven and Tammy Procell are shown behind their dad, Roy, assisting him with the measuring. The water rose faster than expected and covered many trees before they could be harvested. (Courtesy of Solan Procell.)

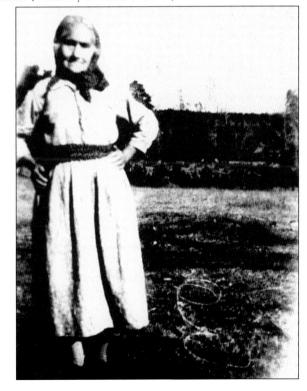

Emma (Morales) Procell, a midwife, brought many children into this world. She was the daughter of Jose De Jesus Morales and Maria Francisca (Menchaca) Manshack. She never had any biological children, but she raised children who had no one to care for them. She was the midwife for the coauthor of this book, Mary Lucille Rivers, and also attended to the birth of Leatha Rivers, the coauthor's mother. (Courtesy of Sally Procell.)

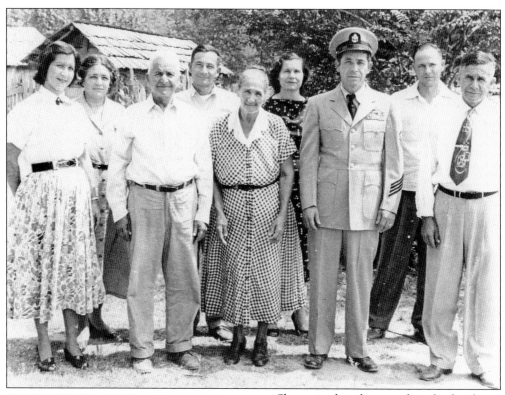

Shown in this photograph is the family of Frank and Juanna Procell. Pictured from left to right are Olivia, Lydia, Frank, Villice, Juanna, Mary, Clifton, Chester, and Ernest. This picture was taken in the 1940s at the home of Frank and Juanna. Their son, Clifton, was stationed at Pearl Harbor during the Japanese attack. He was later captured and became a prisoner of war. (Courtesy of Chester Procell.)

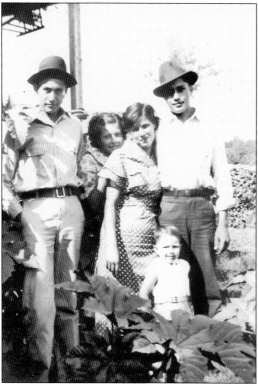

The family of George Remedies is shown taking time to pose for a picture. Pictured from left to right are Jessie, Mary, Verline, Edward, and Johnny Remedies. George was the son of Hosie Antonio Ramirez and Guadalupe Sepulvado. (Photograph courtesy of Ernest Rodrigues.)

In 1958, the Prude Remedies family of Choctaw descent posed for a family picture. Pictured from left to right are (first row) Bill Remedies, Juanna "Janie" Toby, and Prude Remedies; (second row) J. C. "Jay" Remedies, Henrietta "Pete" (Remedies) Bush, Wilma (Remedies) Brown, Levi Remedies, Nancy (Remedies) Rodrigues, and Josephine (Remedies) Solice. (Courtesy of Cody Bruce.)

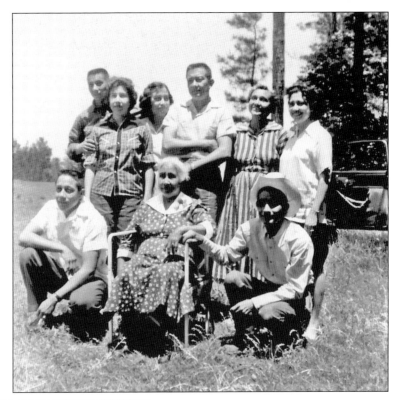

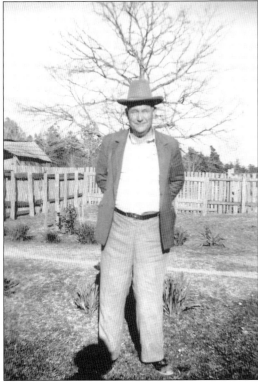

Henry Rivers was the son of Ben Bonaventure and Josephine Rivers. Ben's siblings were Leo, Henry, and Robert. Ben Bonaventure later married Sarah Ann Falcon. Their children are Ethel, Earl, Bessie, Florence, Clarence, Andrew, Melvin, Monroe, and Ruby. (Courtesy of Muriel Rivers.)

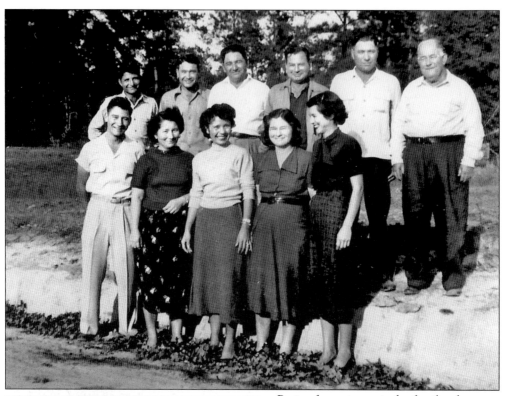

Posing for a picture is the family of Henry and Emma Rivers. They are, from left to right, (first row) Garland, Sylvia Procell, Lovell Renstrom, Grace Sanders, and Josephine White; (second row) Leo, Andrew, Sam A., William, Ben, and father Henry. Henry and Emma were married December 18, 1912, at St. Joseph's Church in Zwolle. (Courtesy of Muriel Rivers.)

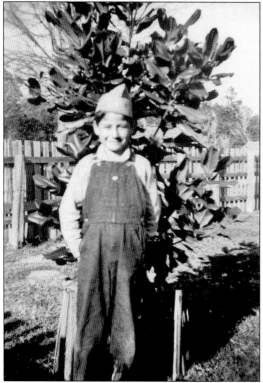

Shown is a young Garland Rivers posing for a picture by the Louisiana state tree, the magnolia. He is the youngest of the 10 children of Henry and Emma Procell Rivers. He married Mary Culver and had three children: Sonya Renee, Joseph Garland, and Wendy Allison. He is the proud grandfather of seven. (Courtesy of Muriel Rivers.)

Andrew "Mooda" Rivers is the son of Henry and Emma Procell Rivers. He married Mary Ann Leone, daughter of Frank Leone and Lena Sepulvado. Their children are Muriel, Anna Jean, Ritta, Kay, Darlene, Scottie, and Ricky. Andrew served in Word War II and took part in the Battle of the Bulge in the European theater. (Courtesy of Muriel Rivers.)

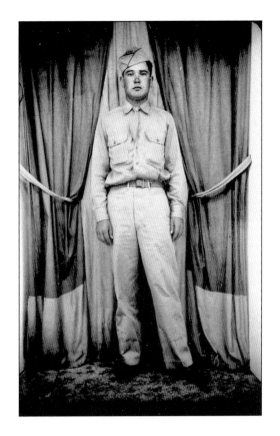

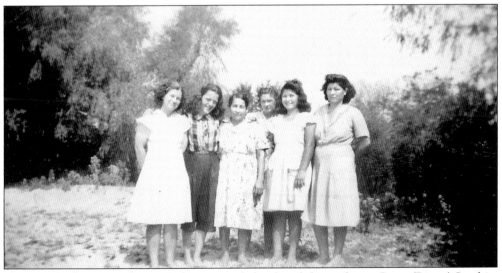

Photographed in September 1947, these pretty ladies from left to right are Grace (Rivers) Sanders, Marilyn Rivers, Mary (Procell) Rivers, Mary Ann (Leone) Rivers, Lovell (Rivers) Renstrom, and Kate (Ebarb) Rivers. Lovell and Grace are daughters of Henry and Emma (Procell) Rivers. Mary (Procell) Rivers was the second wife of Henry Rivers. (Courtesy of Muriel Rivers.)

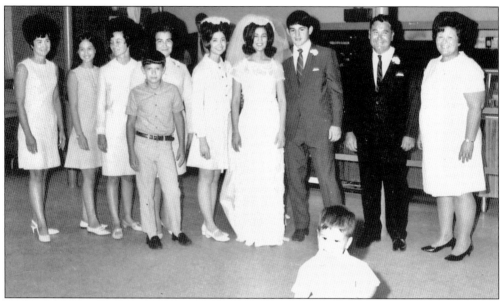

Andrew and Mary Ann Rivers are shown celebrating the marriage of their daughter Darlene to Pat Boudreaux, son of Johnny Boudreaux and Katherine Ebarb. Pictured from left to right are Rita (Rivers) Sepulvado, Scottie (Rivers) Ferguson, Jean (Rivers) Lambert, Ricky Rivers, Muriel Rivers, Kay (Rivers) Stephens, Darlene (Rivers) Boudreaux, Pat Boudreaux, Andrew Rivers, and Mary Ann Rivers. Andrew and Mary Ann's grandson Joseph Sepulvado is shown in the foreground. (Courtesy of Muriel Rivers.)

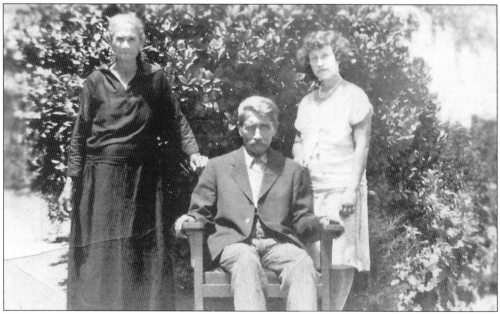

James Richard Rivers (December 1860–April 1936) and Martha Martinez (January 1865–April 1939) are shown with their granddaughter Mary Salinas. Married in April 1877, they became the parents of 15 children, several of whom died at an early age: Samuel, Josephine, Rosie, Richard, Annie, Thomas, Joseph, Mary, John, Steve, Nancy, Lula, George, Lee, and James. Nine of their children preceded them in death. (Courtesy of Mary Lucille Rivers.)

Richard "Dick" Rivers Sr. (July 1881–April 1957) and Elizabeth "Belle" Sepulvado (February 1879–May 1960) were married in February 1901. Dick was one of the first babies baptized at the newly established St. Joseph's Church in 1881. He and Elizabeth had nine children: Clyde, Rosie, Fred, Annie, Thomas, Richard, Leroy, Reasing, and Maggie. (Courtesy of Mary Lucille Rivers.)

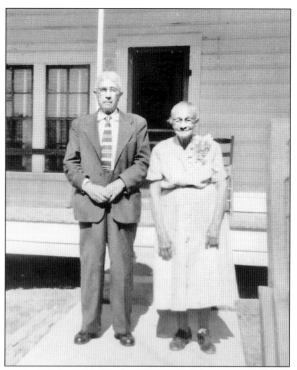

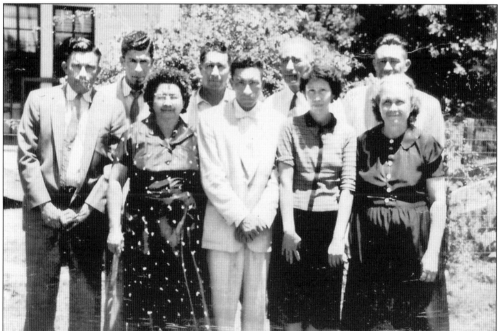

Posing for a picture are the nine children of Dick and Belle Rivers. From left to right are (first row) Jake, Annie, Richard, Maggie, and Rosie; (second row) Reasing, Clyde, Fred "Billy," and Tom. The Rivers family had clear, mathematical minds, with most of the men becoming carpenters or painters. Maggie is the only surviving member as of 2006. All of her brothers and sisters are buried in St. Joseph's Cemetery. (Courtesy of Mary Lucille Rivers.)

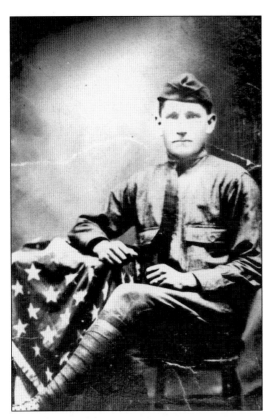

John Rivers, son of Martha Martinez and Richard James Rivers, is shown in uniform and next to the American flag during World War I. He was born May 11, 1891, and died August 28, 1925. He married Ottia Howell; they had one son named John Jr. (Courtesy of Garthe Wright.)

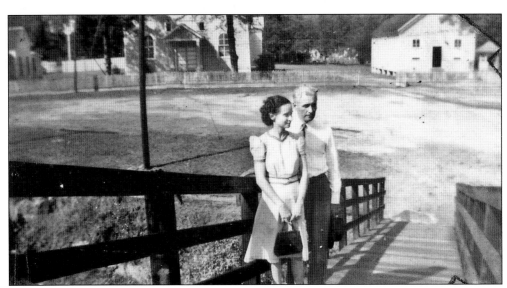

Steve Rivers and Laura Belle Guynes pose on the bridge directly in front of St. Joseph's. In the background behind the picket fence is St. Joseph's Catholic Church. Also pictured is the old school and activities building. Behind the church is the cemetery. (Courtesy of Garthe Wright.)

These men are shown posing for a picture. From left to right are (seated) Louis Sepulvado and ? MacDonald; (standing) Dora Sepulvado and Pete Sepulvado. Louis and Pete were the sons of Pedro and Rosa Lafitte Sepulvado. Dora, son of J. J. and Emily Lafitte Sepulvado, was their cousin. Dora drove the school bus for Ebarb School for 29 years. (Courtesy of Carolyn Williams.)

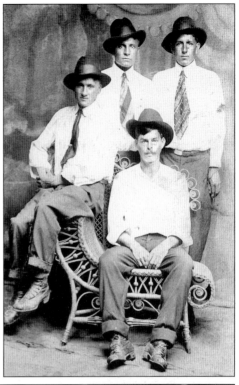

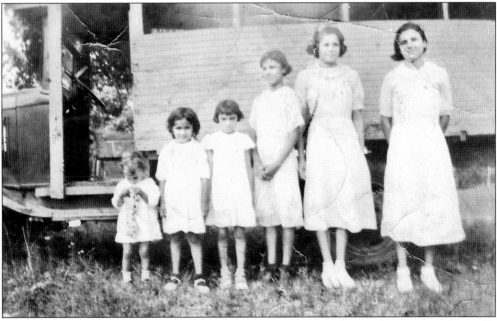

Dora Sepulvado (1894–1986) and Christina Meshell (1896–1986) were the parents of six girls. Pictured from left to right are Elaine, Rosie, Eva, Verna, Janie, and Margie. They posed in front of one of the early school buses that Dora Sepulvado drove to Ebarb School during his 29-year tenure. Sunday mornings would find Dora driving his bus toward St. Joseph's in Zwolle. Anyone walking to church was always welcomed aboard with a big smile. (Courtesy of Margie Rivers.)

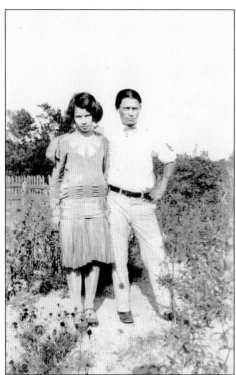

Leatha Rivers poses for a picture in the early 1930s with her cousin, Ellis Ebarb. Everyone had beautiful flowers in their yards. They would let the flowers mature and collect seeds for the next year. Flowers that were easily grown and require little care were crepe myrtles, bachelors buttons, bridal wreath, roses, marigolds or old maids, and prince feathers. (Courtesy of Leonard Ebarb.)

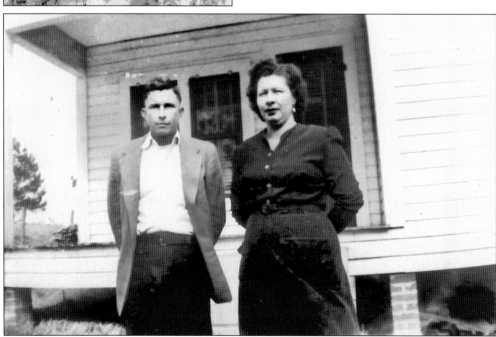

Leroy and Leatha Rivers were married in 1937. Their children are Lucille, Joseph, Roy, Martha, Gary Mark, Nancy, and Steve. They instilled in their children the importance of education. Four of their children became teachers and acquired advanced degrees. Five of their grandchildren obtained college degrees, and three great-grandchildren are in college. (Courtesy of Mary Lucille Rivers.)

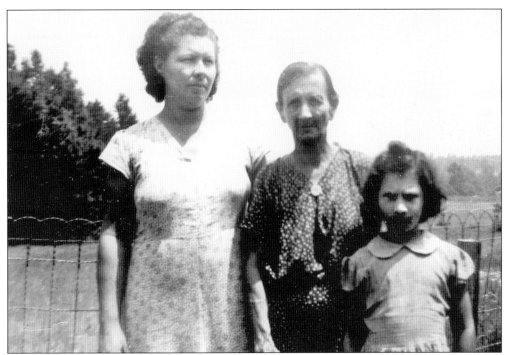

Leatha Rivers (left); her mother, Lucy (Sepulvado) Ebarb; and daughter Martha (Rivers) Henderson pose for a picture in the 1950s. Visiting after Sunday mass was a common thing for them to do. Lucy always had a vegetable garden and beautiful flowers in her yard as long as she was physically able to do so. (Courtesy of Mary Lucille Rivers.)

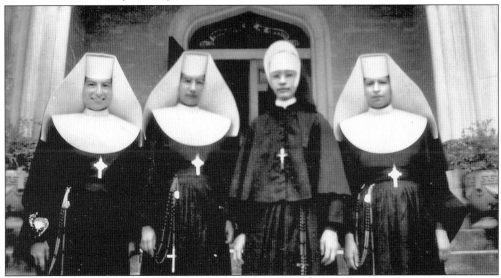

Posing in about 1958 are these four cousins. From left to right are Glenice Rivers, Martinette Rivers, Mary Lucille Rivers, and Jean Ebarb, daughters of Tom, Jake, and Maggie Rivers. Their grandparents were Dick and Belle Rivers. Glenice, Sister Martinette, and Jean were members of the Sisters of the Holy Ghost while Mary Lucille was a member of the Sisters of Divine Providence, all in San Antonio, Texas. Sister Martinette is the only one who remains a nun today. (Courtesy of Mary Lucille Rivers.)

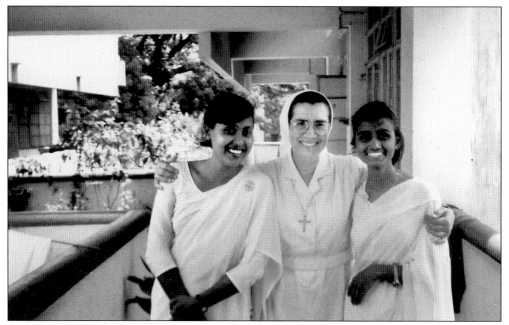

Sr. Martinette Rivers poses with two friends in Bangladesh, where she worked for 15 years. Sister Martinette is now a Sister of Our Lady of Sorrows, whose motherhouse is in Rome. She originally belonged to the Sisters of the Holy Ghost, whose motherhouse is in San Antonio, Texas. The daughter of Tom Rivers and Elizabeth Ebarb, Sister Martinette has been a nun for over 50 years. (Courtesy of Mary Lucille Rivers.)

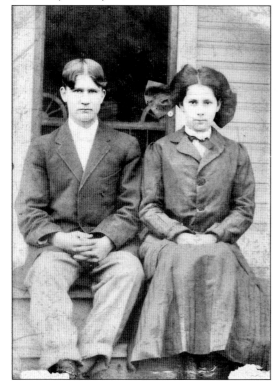

Samuel Henry Rivers (1893–1960) sits with Mary Laroux (1893–1933), whom he would later marry. After her death, he married Ethel Malmay (1914–1991). Sam had two sons with Mary: Sam Henry and Teofilo James. With Ethel, he had two children: Bobby Gene Rivers and Marilyn (Rivers) Sepulvado. (Courtesy of Mary Lucille Rivers.)

116

Jose Esiquio Sepulvado was the son of Jose Antonio Sepulvada and Maria Guadalupe Chavana. He married twice: Rosa Guay then Rebecca Ferguson. At one time, he owned a cotton gin, a gristmill, and many acres that he farmed. He helped build the first Sepulvado School so his children would be able to receive an education. (Courtesy of Mary Lucille Rivers.)

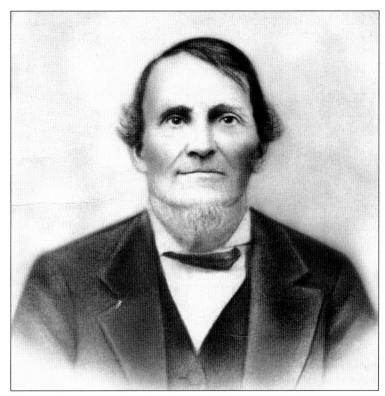

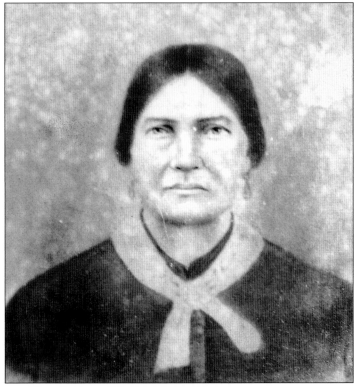

Rosa Guay (1840– c. 1872) was the daughter of Jean Baptiste Guay and Anna Bebee of French and Native American ancestry. She married Jose E. Sepulvado and became the mother of nine children—Elizabeth Isabella, Richard "Desiderio," Maria Justa, Alcario, Juana, Marcelina, Pedro, Joseph, and John. She is buried in the Old Catholic Cemetery. The exact date of her death is unknown. (Courtesy of Cody Bruce.)

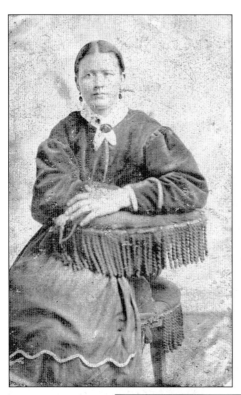

Rebecca Ferguson (March 1859–November 25, 1923) was the daughter of Warrick Ferguson and Maria Gagne of French, English, and Native American ancestry. She first married Jose Caesar Lafitte and had two daughters: Emily and Rosa. Later she married Jose E. Sepulvado and became mother to nine more children: Mary, Henry, John, Joe "Cap," William, James, Lucy, Bettie, and Sam. (Courtesy of Travis Ebarb Jr.)

John H. Sepulvado, born on December 22, 1876, was the son of Jose Esiquio Sepulvado and Rebecca Ferguson. He married Julia Procell, and they had nine children: Della, Jessie, Florence, Emma Lee, Joseph D., Bessie, Mitchell, Raymond, and Cleve. John died December 22, 1969, on his birthday, at the age of 93. (Courtesy of Theresa Sepulvado.)

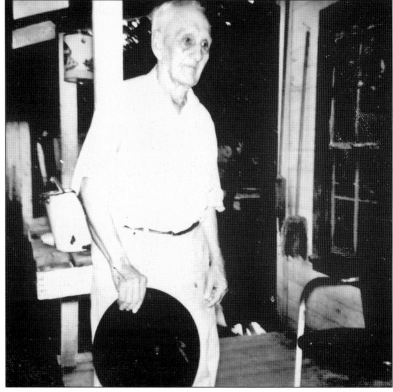

In the picture from left to right are Florence Sepulvado (1905–1994), daughter of John H. and Julie (Procell) Sepulvado, and Walter Malmay (1903–1996), son of Simon Hosea and Juanita (Garcie) Malmay. They were married in 1923. They had the following children: Roy Walter, Ander, Lura Mae, and Rudolph. (Courtesy of Theresa Sepulvado.)

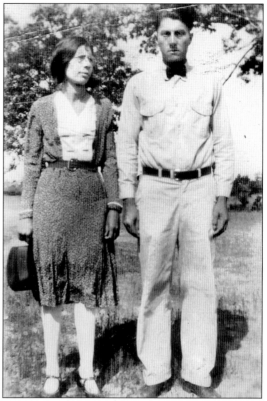

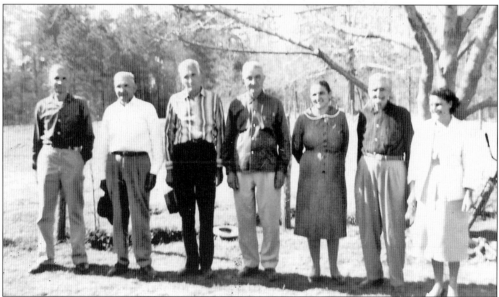

Celebrating his 90th birthday in 1958, Joe the "birthday boy" celebrates with his family. Pictured from left to right are Wesley Sepulvado, Jake Sepulvado, Dora Sepulvado, George Sepulvado, Eva (Sepulvado) Ebarb, Joe, and Mary (Sepulvado) Procell. Joe was born on March 19, 1868, and died in 1966. Good DNA, hard work, and plenty of exercise helped him to live to be almost 100 years old. (Courtesy of Thelma Sepulvado.)

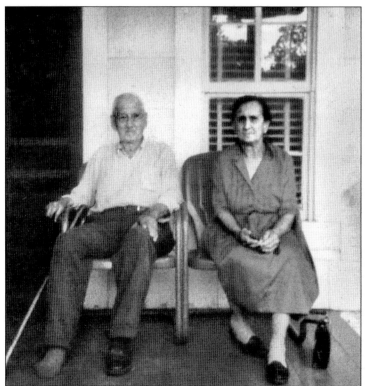

John Sepulvado and Lucy Ebarb pose on the back porch of Lucy's house. Lucy took care of her brothers Jim, Sam, and Cap. Jim and Sam had little houses next to hers and she would cook for them. Her specialties were hot water cornbread, a red pepper soup, collard greens, and baked sweet potatoes. Their other brothers and sisters were Mary, Betty, Henry, Sam, and Will. (Courtesy of Mary Lucille Rivers.)

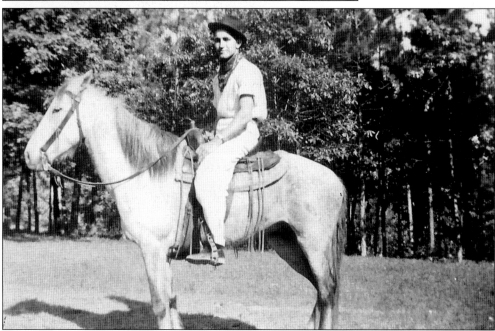

Paul H. Sepulvado (1919–1991) is shown riding a colt from Eli Garcie Sr.'s racehorse. His parents were Paul Sepulvado and Marcelina Martinez. He served in the U.S. Navy in World War II and in Korea. He attained the rank of lieutenant colonel. Paul was also the principal of Ebarb High School in the 1970s. (Courtesy of Theresa Sepulvado.)

Arthur Sepulvado was the son of Oscar Sepulvado and Pearl Meshell. His siblings were Elnora, Zula, and Ethel. Arthur married Creola Procell, daughter of Jim Procell and Louvinia Valentine. Their children are Elizabeth, Stanley, Ricky, Darrell, Charlotte, Shanda, Janice, and Rhonda. They have 20 grandchildren. (Courtesy of Darrell Sepulvado.)

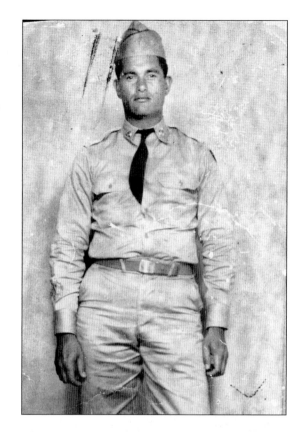

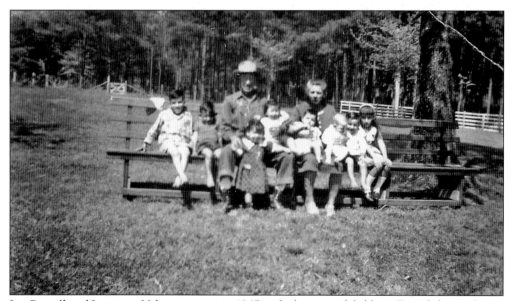

Jim Procell and Louvinia Valentine pose in 1965 with their grandchildren. From left to right are Stanley and Ricky Sepulvado, Jim Procell, Annette Thompson, Charlotte and Shanda Sepulvado, Louvinia, and Janice, Darrell, and Elizabeth Sepulvado. Jim was a sharecropper and logger. Louvinia was a good cook and made great biscuits. (Courtesy of Darrell Sepulvado.)

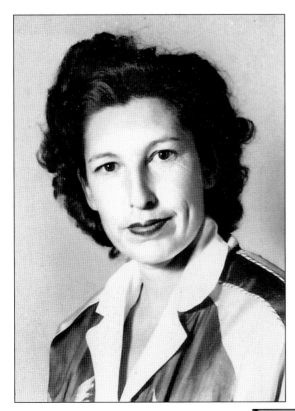

"Mrs. Edith," as she was known by scores of schoolchildren at Ebarb High School, was a lunchroom worker for many years. She was born Edith Margaret Broussard on January 2, 1920. She married Willard Sepulvado (1916–1988), son of Alex Sepulvado and Rosie Ebarb. Her children were Willard Patrick and Bennie Joe. (Courtesy of Jeffery Sepulvado.)

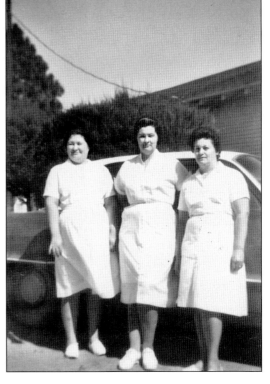

Ebarb School cafeteria workers (cooks), possibly in the early 1970s, are, from left to right, Bernice Garcie, Theresa Sepulvado, and Polly Sepulvado. Ebarb always had a reputation of having the best cafeteria food around. Theresa's uncle Loran Ebarb was principal at the school. (Courtesy of Theresa Sepulvado.)

Stephen Sepulvado (1882–1966) is the son of Richard and Maria Victoria Procell. He married Ascension Garcie (1882–1984). She is the daughter of Jimmy Garcie and Theodore Leone. Their children are Manuel, Sally, Joseph, Nick, Maggie, Cora, Angeline, Blanche, Raymond, Mable, Mattie, and Rosa Lee. Ascension lived to be 102 years old. (Courtesy of Sally Procell.)

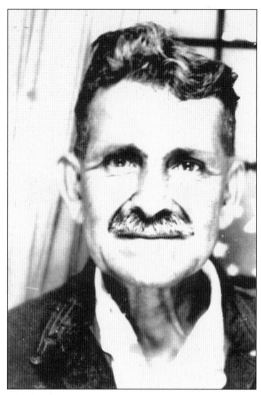

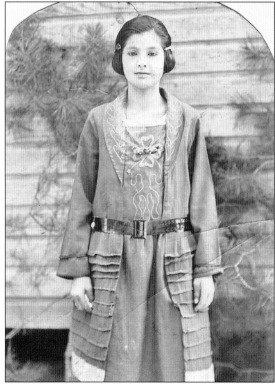

Looking spiffy in her Sunday clothes is Sally Sepulvado, age 16, in 1925. Sally married Edward Procell (1907–1981) and had four children: Edward, Catherine, Louis, and Johnny Ray. Sepulvados have good DNA for longevity as evidenced by Sally being 97 years old and still attending mass every Saturday. (Courtesy of Sally Procell.)

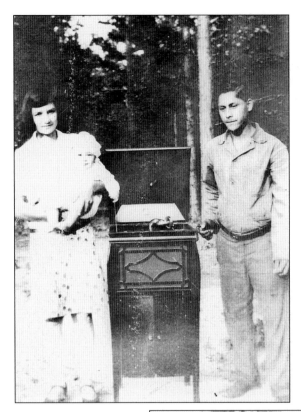

Annie Sepulvado, born September 15, 1913, is the daughter of George Hosea Sepulvado (1882–1967) and Juanna Ebarb (1890–1931). She married Gus Sepulvado (1910–1994), son of Hosea Maria Sepulvado (1867–1935) and Elizabeth (Lizzie) Morales (1873–1913). In the picture, Annie is holding her son Herman; her other children are Jimmy Ray, Bertie Mae, and Linda Faye. Annie, age 93, still attends church services at St. Ann's. (Courtesy of Bertie Mae Malmay.)

Mary Selina Malmay and Frank Sepulvado are shown standing in front of their house. Their children are Bertie, Mattie, Adeline, Martha, Vergaline, Earl, Joseph Vance, and Joseph Paul. Selina always had a garden and beautiful flowers in her yard. She was a faithful member of St. Ann's Circle at St. Joseph Church. (Courtesy of Catherine Sepulvado.)

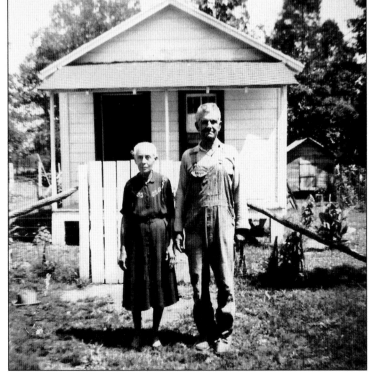

Artie Mae Ebarb is the daughter of Lupie and Lena Ebarb. Lupie's parents are Marceline Ebarb and Maria Sanchez. Lupie was the brother of Fred Ebarb. Artie Mae married Nick Sepulvado (1914–1945), son of Stephen Sepulvado and Ascension Garcie. Nick died in 1945. Nick and Artie Mae's children are Paul Nick, Leroy, Alfred Ralph, and Loretta. Ralph made basketball look easy when he played for the Ebarb Rebels. (Courtesy of Artie Mae [Ebarb] Sepulvado.)

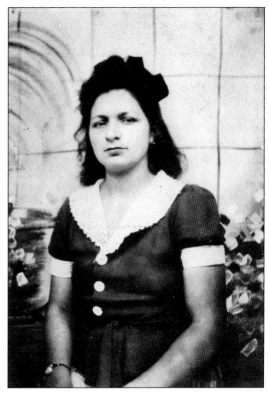

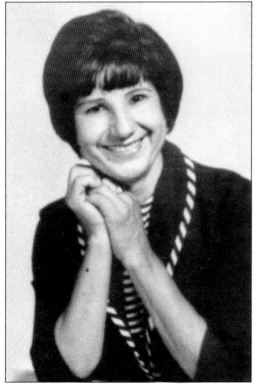

Maggie Sepulvado is shown in her younger days. She is the daughter of Stephen Sepulvado and Ascension Garcie. She married Daniel Manshack, whose parents are George Manschack and Pauline Procell. Maggie and Daniel had one son, Nick Jr., who married Joyce Sepulvado. Maggie was a faithful and caring daughter who took care of her mom, who lived to be 102 years old. (Courtesy of Maggie (Sepulvado) Manshack.)

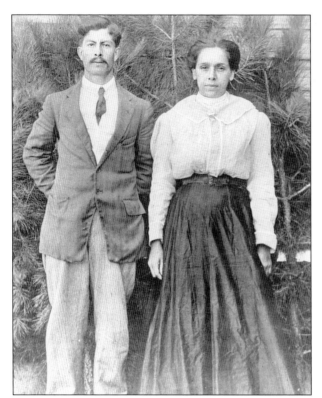

Benjamin "Ben" Knight (1881–1934) is shown with his wife, Gertrude (Trudy) Procell (1879–1958). He had come from Paige, Texas, in the early 1900s with the Procell brothers, Phil and Sam, and their families. They settled in this area and made it their permanent home. Ben and Trudy's children are John, Steve, Eugene, Francis, Jessie, Henry, and Mary. (Courtesy of Eugene Knight.)

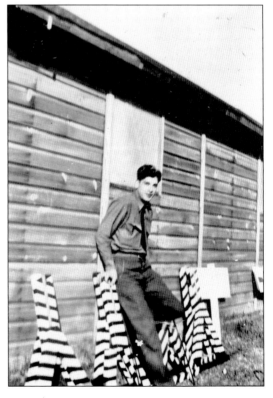

John Knight as a young man worked in the Civilian Conservation Corps, which was a part of the New Deal Program in 1933. It provided training and employment for the conservation of natural resources. They planted trees, built dams, and fought forest fires. More than two million men served in the corps before Congress abolished it in 1942. (Courtesy of Pauline Ebarb.)

Alene Wright is standing next to her father, George Washington Rivers. Her mother died, and her father was left to raise the children during the Depression years. Alene was a pillar of the church at St. John's in Many. Her church, her family, and her genealogy work were important parts of her life. (Courtesy of Garthe Wright.)

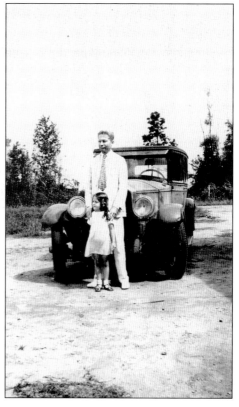

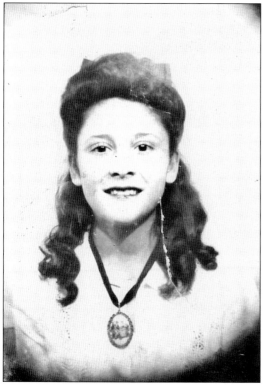

Alene, daughter of George Washington Rivers and Sally Mae Holder, was born on May 4, 1928, and died on April 14, 2005, after a lingering battle with cancer. Spending over 20 years researching tribal families, Alene was designated Tribal Genealogist in 1997. Alene frequented libraries, courthouses, and cemeteries in her search for information. (Courtesy of Garthe Wright.)

ACROSS AMERICA, PEOPLE ARE DISCOVERING SOMETHING WONDERFUL. *THEIR HERITAGE.*

Arcadia Publishing is the leading local history publisher in the United States. With more than 3,000 titles in print and hundreds of new titles released every year, Arcadia has extensive specialized experience chronicling the history of communities and celebrating America's hidden stories, bringing to life the people, places, and events from the past. To discover the history of other communities across the nation, please visit:

www.arcadiapublishing.com

Customized search tools allow you to find regional history books about the town where you grew up, the cities where your friends and family live, the town where your parents met, or even that retirement spot you've been dreaming about.

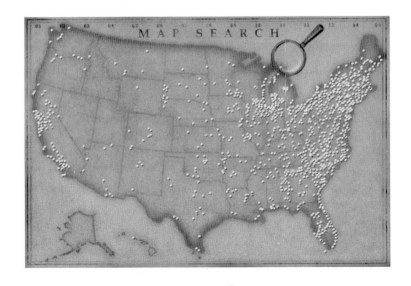